Dictionary of Modern English Grammar

Grammar, syntax and style for the 21st century

Compiled by
NED HALLEY

Wordsworth Reference

For customers interested in other titles from
Wordsworth Editions visit out website at
www.wordsworth-editions.com

For our latest list and a full mail-order service contact
Bibliophile Books, 5 Thomas Road, London E14 7BN

Tel: +44 0207 515 9222   Fax: +44 0207 538 4115
e-mail: orders@bibliophilebooks.com

First published 2005 by Wordsworth Editions Limited
8B East Street, Ware, Hertfordshire SG12 9HJ

ISBN 1 84022 308 1

Typeset by Antony Gray
Printed and bound in Great Britain by
Mackays of Chatham, Chatham, Kent

For my daughter
LYDIA

A BRIEF WORD

"The greatest work of art ever created by the human race."
BERNARD LEVIN (1928–2004)
on the English language

English is the global language of the 21st century. A quarter of the planet's population is conversant, and it is the most widely taught second language in schools worldwide. It is a common bond between more than a billion people, thanks partly to the legacy of empire, but increasingly to the spread of Anglo-American influence of a thoroughly modern kind.

More than any other language, English evolves. New words, and new meanings for old words, are added by the score every year, and faithfully added to succeeding editions of the *Oxford English Dictionary*. There are well over 600,000 words already, equipping English with by far the largest vocabulary of any language.

Equally awesome is the variety of English. As represented by the accents of Clydeside, or the pidgin of east Asia, or the street idiom of American cities, it can sound like an entirely different language in each location.

But the standard form of English is always the touchstone. While differing nationalities, cultures and cliques might have their own distinctive dialects, the core language remains a point of reference for all. This is especially true of written English.

And it is to the standard form of written English that this book is dedicated. It is, quite simply, an aid to writing the language in the way that the greatest number of people will understand.

This is a subjective guide to English as it is being used at this early stage of the 21st century. But it is also a reminder of how the language arrived at this point. English is largely rooted in ancient Greek and Latin, and to grasp this is, I believe, a key to understanding how modern English works, and how we can use it to the best effect.

I have included here the basics of grammar, punctuation and spelling. There is guidance on difficult words and fashionable words, on the use of slang and the necessity of avoiding clichés. Much of the book is devoted to the nuts and bolts of the language, but there is much, too, on the colourful origins of that immense vocabulary and the conventions by which we put the words in order.

This book is primarily about making use of the language now. But if it also arouses the reader's interest in where English came from, and where it might be heading next, it will have more than done its job.

NED HALLEY, 2005

A

a First letter of the alphabet – in most alphabets as well as in English – and the indefinite article. 'A' comes to English from Etruscan, the Italian language that preceded the Latin of Rome. Greek, also a language older than Latin, had *alpha* as its first letter, as did the Semitic languages with *aleph* and *alph* – which meant 'ox' (a castrated bull as a beast of burden). Some experts claim that the Semitic letter 'a' resembled the outline of a bull's head.

a and **an** A becomes 'an' when preceding a word with an initial vowel or vowel sound (as in honest, honour and hour). But there can be difficulties over some words beginning with 'h.' Which is correct – a hotel, or an hotel? The origin of the confusion is that the word hotel was formerly pronounced 'otel' because it comes directly from French. Other words borrowed from French have caused similar problems – habitué, hors d'oeuvre. It is certainly correct to precede these with 'an' if the initial letter is not pronounced. But it is no more than an affectation to place 'an' before straightforward English words with a stressed 'h.' To write 'an historian' makes no more sense than to write 'an history.'

a– As a prefix, for example in amoral and asexual and as **an–** in anarchy or anaemia, 'a' and 'an' denote the negation of the sense in the main word. Thus amoral means devoid of morality, asexual means having no gender, anarchy means without government or order and anaemia describes the absence or shortage of red corpuscles in the blood. From the Greek prefix *a* (not or without).

@ Typographic symbol for 'at' now universally recognised via its use in e-mail and website addresses.

abbreviation The tendency to shorten words and phrases has always had as much to do with the identification of groups as it has with the convenience of brevity. That most scholarly élite, the graduate body of Cambridge University, identifies its alumni by allowing them to place the mysterious word 'Cantab' after the initials of their degree honour, recalling *Cantabrigiensis*, the town's Roman name – which had been out of use for at least 500 years before the University's foundation in the 13th century.

But less-exclusive groups are equally keen on abbreviation. When teenagers of the 1960s began to adopt 'fab' (from fabulous) they were doing so as a badge of generation. Parents deplored the word's triteness and thus made it all the more relishable for their children to use it. Even today, anyone of advanced years using the now-ironic 'fab' tends to sound ridiculous, because the word still somehow belongs to the young.

Some abbreviations are ephemeral. Ammo (from ammunition) did not long survive the Second World War and infra dig (from Latin *infra dignitatem* meaning beneath one's dignity) faded long before the 21st century. But some become words in their own right, sometimes effectively replacing their progenitors: bra, gym, pub, taxi, vet.

ablative   In grammar, the 'case' of a noun or pronoun expressed in the context of location, direction, time or other influences. In the sentence "She sat next to him", the pronoun "him" is in the ablative case. As a determinant of word forms, ablative is not a distinct case in English. In Latin, where nouns, pronouns and adjectives are 'declined' into cases, ablative is the final case in the sequence nominative, vocative, accusative, genitive, dative, ablative.

able   When to use "I am able to" in preference to "I can"? There is rarely any reason to do so other than for deliberate effect and usually in the negative, as in "I am completely unable to make sense of what you are saying" as more forceful than "I cannot make sense … "

-able and **-ible**   Adjectival suffix with variations that can prove a problem to remember. Words with the respective endings usually follow their Latin origins, as capable from *capabilis* and horrible from *horribilis*. Words formed from Latin verbs, such as amiable from *amare* (to love) and audible from *audire* (to hear) dependably follow the original conjugation (*qv*) but there are no other consistent rules to the correct spelling.

There are many more adjectives suffixed with -able than with -ible. Following are selections from both groups:

acceptable	correctable	guessable
accountable	creditable	habitable
actionable	culpable	hangable
adaptable	curable	honourable
adjustable	debatable	hospitable
adorable	demonstrable	imaginable
allowable	dependable	immovable
amenable	deplorable	immutable
amiable	desirable	impeccable
amicable	despicable	impenetrable
applicable	detachable	imperturbable
appreciable	detectable	implacable
approachable	detestable	impregnable
arable	dispensable	impressionable
arguable	disposable	imprisonable
arrestable	disputable	imputable
attainable	durable	inalienable
attributable	eatable	inconceivable
available	educable	incurable
bankable	enforceable	indefatigable
bearable	equable	indescribable
believable	excitable	indictable
biddable	excusable	indispensable
breakable	expandable	indistinguishable
calculable	expendable	inestimable
capable	fashionable	inevitable
certifiable	flammable	inexcusable
changeable	foreseeable	inexorable
chargeable	forgettable	inexplicable
clubbable	forgivable	inextricable
comfortable	gaugeable	inflammable
conceivable	gettable	inflatable
connectable	governable	inimitable
consolable	gradable	inoperable
contestable	graspable	inscrutable

-able and -ible

inseparable
insufferable
insuperable
insupportable
insurmountable
intolerable
intractable
iviolable
irreconcilable
irrefutable
irreplaceable
justifiable
knowledgeable
laughable
likeable
lovable
malleable
manageable
manoeuvrable
marriageable
measurable
memorable
miserable
modifiable
mootable
movable
mutable
nameable
navigable
negotiable
notable
noticeable
numerable
objectionable
observable
obtainable
offerable
operable

palatable
palpable
pardonable
passable
payable
peaceable
pensionable
perceivable
perishable
permeable
personable
pleasurable
potable
predictable
preferable
presentable
preventable
probable
profitable
programmable
prosecutable
provable
publishable
pullable
punishable
pursuable
qualifiable
quantifiable
questionable
quotable
rateable
readable
reasonable
recognizable
reconcilable
rectifiable
redeemable
regrettable

reliable
renewable
reputable
retractable
sackable
saleable
sellable
serviceable
sizeable
sociable
solvable
squeezable
storable
stretchable
suitable
sustainable
targetable
testable
taxable
teachable
tolerable
traceable
tractable
tradable
transferable
transplantable
traversable
treasonable
treatable
triable
unassailable
unconscionable
undeniable
understandable
unexceptionable
unflappable
unhelpable
unimpeachable

unmentionable
unmissable
unmistakable
unnameable
unpalatable
unplayable
unprintable
unpronounceable
unshakeable
unshiftable
unshockable
unsinkable
unspeakable
unthinkable
untouchable
untraceable
unutterable
usable
valuable
variable
venerable
viable
viewable
voidable
vulnerable
walkable
warrantable
washable
watchable
wearable
wipable

accessible
admissible
audible
collapsible

combustible
compatible
comprehensible
contemptible
convertible
credible
deductible
dirigible
discernible
divisible
edible
extensible
fallible
feasible
flexible
forcible
gullible
horrible
illegible
imperceptible
implausible
impossible
impressible
inaccessible
inadmissible
incompatible
incomprehensible
incorrigible
incredible
indefensible
indelible
indestructible
indigestible
indivisible
ineligible
inexhaustible
inexpressible

infallible
inflexible
insensible
insuppressible
intangible
intelligible
invincible
invisible
irascible
irrepressible
irresistible
irresponsible
irreversible
legible
negligible
ostensible
perceptible
perfectible
permissible
plausible
possible
reducible
reprehensible
resistible
responsible
reversible
risible
sensible
submersible
submissible
suggestible
susceptible
tangible
terrible
transfusible
transmissible
visible

abled

abled   Recent term denoting capacity for general or specific activities, particularly where contrasted with disabled, as in "the resort has many attractions for abled and disabled visitors alike."

ableism   Discrimination favouring able-bodied people over the disabled. "The shop's refusal to install entry ramps was denounced as ableist."

abridge   To shorten a story or script. An abridged book is one reduced in length from the first published edition.

abscission   Figure of speech in which a sentence is left incomplete, although the meaning remains clear, as in the expression of astonishment "What the ... " Latin *abscindere* (to cut off).

absolutely   Intensive affirmative used to denote emphatic agreement or, as "absolutely not," emphatic disagreement. The word absolute, meaning independent or unconditional, comes from Latin *absolvere* (to set free). Now overused. Avoid, unless absolutely necessary.

absolute superlative   Figure of speech. It is the use of a superlative to accord high praise rather than to assert that the object in mind is truly the best, biggest or whatever. Examples are "You do say the kindest things" and "I had the strangest experience."

abstract   It is a verb meaning to take away, from Latin *abs* (away from) and *trahere* (to pull) but it is as an adjective that abstract presents us with one of the most difficult common words in the language. In the familiar phrase 'abstract art' just what does it mean? Describing the abstract art of the 20th century, in particular the apparently random 'expressionist' work of artists such as Jackson Pollock (who literally threw his paint at the canvas and earned the name "Jack the Dripper" from one sneering reviewer) the word is understood to mean paintings with no recognisable form – as distinct from a figurative picture of a person or place, object or event. But the sense of abstract has now been extended into wider realms of philosophy, as if there were some lines of thought that can be called figurative as distinct from others that are abstract. Thus, democracy is abstract but democratic government is tangible. But these distinctions are more sensibly drawn as theoretical versus practical. Terms such as 'abstract concept' and 'abstract idea' are commonly used, but really the word is redundant, because ideas and concepts by their very nature are abstract rather than figurative or concrete.

absurd, theatre of the   A phrase beloved of theatre critics, it derives from a distinct period in the history of drama, the years immediately after the Second World War. Playwrights led by Samuel Beckett and Eugene Ionesco adopted the principles of farce to put their characters in ridiculous situations in which tragedy always lurked uncomfortably in the shadows, evoking the insane suspension of routine life that is imposed by all-pervading war.

accent   In poetry and music, it is a syllable or note given emphasis by stress or pitch. In speaking, it is an identifiable style of pronunciation, as in a Geordie (Tyneside) accent, an upper-class accent or a foreign accent.

In the written word, accents are a form of punctuation more common in French, German, Spanish and other major languages than in English. But when using some imported words, it is often helpful to include their indigenous accents. Café without the accent is in danger of being taken as intended in the jocular pronunciations 'kayf' or 'kaff' and fiancé looks unpronounceably odd without its accent. Following are examples of the principal accents in use.

> après (as in après-ski) – *grave* (French, pronounced
>   'grahv') accent
> café – acute accent
> château – circumflex
> Fraülein – umlaut (German for English diaeresis)
> garçon – cedilla
> mañana – tilda
> naïf – diaeresis

accusative   In grammar the case of a noun or pronoun as the object of a sentence. In the sentence "I hit him" I is in the nominative case and him is in the accusative case.

acronym   A word formed from a sequence of initials. The world at present is gripped in an outbreak of acronymania (a morbid tendency to form and use acronyms) as commercial and public institutions invent ever more contrived names for themselves, their products, their target markets, even for related abstract concepts.

The present craze dates from the 1970s, when nuclear-weapons negotiations between the United States and the former Soviet Union were daily in the headlines. Summits to discuss proliferation of ICBMs (intercontinental ballistic missiles) were given a series of acronymous names including SALT, Strategic Arms Limitation Talks, and START, Strategic Arms Reduction Talks.

Popular media-generated acronyms followed, creating new words now firmly installed in the dictionaries. Included were the yuppies of 1982, the reviled but envied Young Urban (or Upwardly mobile) Professionals of American cities. Other social stereotypes have followed: the envied, wealthy, carefree dink(y) couple – double income, no kids (yet) – and the bigoted environmental activist the nimby – not in my backyard.

Some acronyms are rather looser renderings of their constituent initials, for example London's 'Footsie' share index, derived from the Financial Times Stock Exchange index or FTSE and 'Neddy' from the UK's National Economic Development Council (NEDC).

The acronym habit is particularly prevalent in medicine, with many newly identified diseases given names readily reducible to initials. Bovine spongiform encephalopathy ('mad cow' disease) is known universally as BSE and its human counterpart, variant Creutzfeldt-Jakob disease, as CJD or more precisely vCJD. Some disease names appear to have been contrived in order to create a memorable acronym – such as AIDS (acquired immune-deficiency syndrome, now so commonplace it can be written as 'Aids') and SAD (seasonal-affected disorder).

The UK's medically based anti-tobacco body goes under the neat acronym ASH (Action on Smoking and Health), while the title adopted by its opposing lobby group, FOREST, is rather more cumbersome; it stands for Freedom Organisation for the Right to Enjoy Smoking Tobacco. Other acronymous organisations might well have cause to regret their choice of name. Anti-abortion group the Society for the Protection of the Unborn Child, sometimes rendered in mischievous sections of the media as SPUNC, is a case in point.

Many well-established acronyms have become fully integrated into the language. Examples include laser (light amplification by stimulated emission of radiation), quango (quasi-autonomous non-governmental organisation) and radar (radio detection and ranging).

Greek *akron* (end) and *onoma* (name).

acrostics

> **a**re playful
> **c**ontrivances of prose or verse,
> **r**endered so that each line
> **o**pens or closes with words in
> **s**equence to read from
> **t**op to bottom, their
> **i**nitial or final letters
> **c**onstituting a word or phrase.

Known in Roman literature, acrostics have been composed by poets including Geoffrey Chaucer (1345–1400). From Greek *akron* (end) and *stichos* (line).

act A major section of a play or opera.

active and **passive**   In grammar a verb is in the 'active voice' when it describes an action by the subject of the phrase; as, "he gave her the flowers." When the verb describes an action affecting the object of the phrase, it is in the passive voice; as, "she received the flowers from him."

acute accent   In words adopted into English from foreign languages, particularly French, the acute accent is the one that rises from left to right. On the letter 'e', it replaces a following 's' from former times, indicating an appropriate emphasis in pronunciation. In French *cliché* and Spanish *olé!* it is clearly vital to write the accent, and it is good practice to be consistent. Note that in the default dictionary provided with Microsoft Windows software, words including café and cliché are spelled with the accent – surely a sign that these punctuation marks are here to stay.

adaptation   the reworking of one medium into an another, as an adaptation of a novel as a film, or a television series as an adaptation of a biography or historical work.

adapter or **adaptor**   One who adapts, or an apparatus for connecting multiple electric plugs. Both spellings are equally acknowledged, but there is some argument for using adaptor for the appliance and adapter for a person adapting.

addendum   The term for material added to the text of a book, usually at the last minute in the production process. It's the gerund (*qv*) of Latin *addere*. Correct plural is in the Latin form, addenda.

address   A formal speech or, as a verb, to speak formally. Using the word address implies the speechmaker has prepared the words with care and that they convey importance – perhaps pomposity. Queen Victoria is reputed to have complained that her least-favourite prime minister, William Gladstone, "addresses us as if we were a public meeting."

adjective   Part of speech. An adjective is a word used to qualify a noun, adding information or comment as, respectively, an old man or a wicked man. From Latin *adjectivum* (*nomen*), an added (word). It is an axiom of good speaking and writing that adjectives should only be used when truly necessary. In his 2002 memorial eulogy to former cabinet minister Barbara Castle, Foreign Secretary Jack Straw recalled her remark, "Bugger the adjectives. It's the nouns and verbs people want."

Advent   In Christian tradition, the season before Christmas, beginning with the fourth Sunday before 25 December. Latin *adventus* (arrival).

adverb   Part of speech. An adverb qualifies a verb, modifying meaning, as "she rose *painfully* from the chair." From Latin *ad* (to) and *verbum* (word, verb).

adviser or **advisor**   Both spellings are used, but dictionaries give adviser as the one in most common use.

Aeschylean   Describes the kind of portentous writing characterised by the first of ancient Greece's great tragic poets,

Aeschylus (525–456BC). Aeschylus's own life was as epic as his verse plays. He served in the Athenian armies that defeated the Persians in the two great battles of Marathon and Salamis – conflicts which did much to determine the course of history – and wrote on themes of appropriately grand dimension. He is most remembered for the *Oresteia*, a three-part drama about the murder of mythical king Agamemnon. Aeschylus is, in effect, the father of tragedy. He is said, however, to have died in what now seem comical circumstances. He was on holiday in Sicily when an eagle, far above, dropped a tortoise on his bald head.

affect and **effect** As verbs, these words are distinct and not interchangeable. To affect is to influence, as in "bad diet affects children's behaviour." To effect is to cause or bring about, as in "an improved diet might effect an improvement in children's behaviour." As a noun, affect is now rare. Use effect.

Afrikaans Note the spelling of the language spoken by South Africans of Dutch descent, known as Afrikaners (who have one 'a', not two).

Afro-Caribbean Now common for black populations known, or perceived to be, descendants of slaves taken from Africa to the American and British colonies of the Caribbean.

Aga saga A genre of popular fiction so-called after the cookers favoured by the British middle classes. The term was coined in ironic recollection of the 'kitchen-sink sagas' of 1950s novels and drama centred on mundane post-war domestic life. It suggests stories of family life amid rural comforts, punctuated by fleeting infidelities and trivial material crises. The first writer to be branded in this way was Joanna Trollope, who remains a leading practitioner and is reputed strongly to dislike having her work thus described.

agenda Buzz word. It means a list of things to do or discuss, usually at a meeting or conference, deriving from the Latin verb *agere* (to do). But it has been adopted in business and politics as a loose term for anything from a policy to a conspiracy, as in the House of Commons statement made by an opposition spokesman on 2002 government proposals to put private companies in charge of failing hospitals: "A cunning plan by the Prime Minister to regain the agenda on the Health Service." In effect, a remark devoid of any meaning whatsoever. Agenda should be ruthlessly avoided in any context other than its true one.

Age of Reason Vague and much misunderstood description of a period in English life, and described in contemporary and subsequent literature. It starts with the Restoration of the English monarchy in 1660 and continues into the greater part of the 18th century. 'Reason' as opposed to political and religious dogma dictated the direction of the arts, and the values of decency and restraint were upheld.

Agitprop Twentieth-century word directly derived from Russian *Agitpropbyuro*, the former Soviet office of agitation and propaganda. Agitprop used in the historical context as official communist propaganda is written with an initial capital. In a general sense, use lower case.

Aids Now an acceptable rendering of AIDS, or acquired immune-deficiency syndrome.

aka Abbreviation for 'also known as.'

alexandrine From the time of the Renaissance in France, beginning in the late 15th century, all formal poetry was written in 12-syllable lines known as alexandrines. It was a revival of a classical style of prosody (poetic structure) used in an immortal verse written 300 years earlier, the *Roman d'Alexandre* – the story of Alexander the Great, the Macedonian king who conquered all the known world in ancient times. It is an insight into the seriousness with which the French take their poetry that when Victor Hugo's play, *Hernani*, opened in Paris in 1830, the audience rioted when they discovered it did not conform to the alexandrine line – until then universal in mainstream drama. The alexandrine equates to the iambic pentameter (*qv*) of English literature.

alien It means foreign (from Latin *alienus*) rather than specifically extraterrestrial.

allegory A story with meanings on two levels. *Aesop's Fables* are among the best-known allegories in literature. A good example is the tale of the fox who fails to reach the tempting bunch of grapes hanging from a vine because he can neither reach nor jump high enough, and dismisses them as probably sour anyway. The story has its literal meaning, plus its allegorical meaning: an illustration of the human tendency to disdain what we cannot afford or achieve – thus the expression 'sour grapes.' Latin *allegoria* (speaking otherwise).

alliteration   Figure of speech in which phrases are formed from words beginning with the same letters. It is a form beloved of newspaper headline writers – 'Booming Britain Breeds Bounciest Babies' – and is a mainstay of tongue twisters: Round the rugged rock the ragged rascal ran. Originally in English literature it was a device in poetry, a form said to pre-date even rhyming. Latin *ad* (in addition to) and *littera* (letter).

all right   It is not all right to write this phrase as 'alright.'

All Souls   Roman Catholic day of prayer for souls in Purgatory (*qv*) – 2 November.

allspice   Not, as commonly believed, a culinary condiment mixed from several different plants, but a product solely of the pimento – and so known for its composite aroma redolent of cinnamon, cloves and nutmeg.

allude   It means to refer, usually indirectly, as in "the poem alludes to the horror of war." Beware confusing allude with 'elude' meaning to escape. Also beware mixing up 'allusion' meaning reference with 'illusion' meaning a mistaken belief.

almanac   In book form, a calendar of events. Also a compendium of statistical and other information, usually published yearly. Occasionally, and archaically, spelt almanack.

alphabet   The word comes from the first two letters of the Greek alphabet, *alpha*, *beta*, but our alphabet is the Roman one, derived from Etruscan – Italy's dominant civilisation before the rise of Rome – and ultimately from characters first formed by writers in the Middle East long before 1,000BC. The first alphabets consisted only of consonants but the Latinised Etruscan version had all the letters of today except j, u and w, added in the Middle Ages.

alternate and alternative

alternate and **alternative** As an adjective, alternate means every other, as in 'she worked alternate days.' Alternative describes something subject to choice or preference, as in 'she was offered a red jumper or an alternative in green.' Alternative has lately come to signify parallel and subversive movements in the arts, such as alternative comedy – distinguished by a bemusing blend of political correctness (no sexist or racist jokes) and foul language.

am and **pm** They abbreviate *ante meridiem* and *post meridiem*, Latin for before midday and after midday. It is now common to use them without stops or spaces; as 9.30am rather than 9.30 a.m.

amateur Now much used as a pejorative, denoting a person lacking skill in any occupation or activity. But it continues to apply to that dying breed of enthusiasts who partake in sports, hobbies or pastimes for their own pleasure, as distinct from 'professionals' undertaking the same activities for payment. Originally, an amateur was a lover of, and by implication a casual expert on, any pleasurable occupation or cultural activity. Latin *amator* (lover).

Amazon There is no connection between the great river of South America and the fearsome female warriors of ancient Scythia, whose name means 'breastless' from Greek *a-* (no) and *mazos* (breast). Write in lower case when using metaphorically, as in "an amazon athlete."

ambiguous and **ambivalent** Beware confusion. Ambiguous means doubtful or unclear in sense, as in "an ambiguous remark." Ambivalent means a state of mind confused by conflicting emotions, as in "he was ambivalent about joining in."

America As a shortening of the United States of America it is inadequate, because America can be taken to mean all of the American continent incorporating Canada and Latin America. The name America is derived from that of Italian-born Spanish explorer Amerigo Vespucci (1451–1512), who first landed in Venezuela in 1499 and whose Latinised name, Americus, was adopted by map-makers after he became Spain's senior official navigator.

American English   It is by now well known that many of the spellings unique to American English are in fact 18th-century British English. Why American English has not evolved in line with its British begetter is a mystery. And what is even more puzzling is that so few American spellings have successfully remigrated into British English. When quoting American proper names, it is correct to use the indigenous spelling – Department of Defense, World Trade Center – but the problem is that the words can look like misspellings. In this respect, treat American English as if it were a foreign language, and convert the words into British English, just in the way we render proper names from, say, Italian: Milan from Milano, Turin from Torino.

There are hundreds of words that are spelled differently on either side of the Atlantic, and below are some examples, some representing groups of words, with the British English placed first.

     aesthete – esthete
     analogue – analog, also dialogue – dialog etc
     calibre – caliber
     centre – center, also metre – meter etc
     cheque – check, chequered – checkered etc
     colour – color, flavour – flavor etc
     defence – defense, also offence – offense etc
     foetus – fetus
     grey – gray
     manoeuvre – maneuver
     marshal – marshall
     mould – mold
     paralyse – paralyze, also analyse – analyze etc
     programme – program

amount   Beware misuse of the word amount, particularly in confusion with 'number.' An amount is a quantity of a given material or concept – thus an amount of money or an amount of time. A number is a quantity made up of individual units, either material or abstract – thus a number of people or a number of opportunities. It is bad English to say 'a great amount of people,' just as it is nonsense to say, 'a great number of money.'

amour propre

amour propre   Old-fashioned French term that persists in the more decorous backwaters of written English. It means self love or self esteem.

anachronism   Something abstract or material that is, or seems, out of its time, as in "his courtly manners were an anachronism." The term is widely used now in a pejorative sense, as in "hunting with dogs is an anachronism." In literature, anachronism can be used deliberately for effect. Perhaps the famous example is in Shakespeare's *Julius Caesar*, in which a town clock chimes the hour in Rome – 1400 years before a public clock was established anywhere in the world (the first was in Milan, Italy, in 1353). Unfortunately, not all anachronism in literature is deliberate. Authors of all periods have been and remain prone to describing modes of speech, behaviour and dress – as well as material topics – that are hopelessly out of their time. Greek *ana* (backwards) and *khronos* (time).

anacoluthon   A grammatical oddity where sense is ambiguous, as "while at work, Mr Smith's dog escaped." This is supposed to convey the sense that the owner of the dog was at work while the pet was escaping, but could well be taken to mean that the dog itself was at work at the time it escaped. Avoid such anacoluthons! In the example, the phrase would be better written, "while Mr Smith was at work, his dog escaped."

anagram   Beloved of crossword compilers and solvers, a word or phrase formed by rearranging the letters of other words, as pot and opt are anagrams of top. Greek *ana* (backwards) and *gramma* (letter).

analogue   In information technology, a continuously variable physical display, as in an analogue speedometer as distinct from a digital one. Greek *analogos* (proportionate).

analogy   In philology (*qv*) the forming of inflections in words that imitate those in other words rather than following known construction from the words' origins. In a more general sense, an analogy is also a literary device, comparing distinct objects or concepts to illustrate meaning, as the triumphs and disasters of football presented by a sports writer as an analogy of life itself. Green *analogos* (proportionate).

anaphora Figure of speech. There are two forms. One is the repetition of a word or phrase to begin a succession of clauses of sentences, as in Alfred, Lord Tennyson's poem The Charge of the Light Brigade (1854): 'Theirs not to make reply, Theirs not to reason why, Theirs but to do and die.' Secondly, anaphora is the avoidance of the repetition of a word within a sentence, as "I work in a bank and so does my wife." Greek *ana* (back) and *phero* (to bear).

anarchy Originally, a state of disorder caused by absence of government, but more recently any condition of chaos. Greek *an* (without) and *arkhos* (ruler).

anastrophe Figure of speech in which usual order of words is reversed for effect, as "mad is the world" instead of "the world is mad." Greek *ana* (back) and *strepho* (to turn).

anathema Object of detestation. It is an abstract word, so don't qualify it with the indefinite article. Say "politics was anathema to him" not "politics was an anathema to him." Greek *anathema* (a thing accursed).

and The main connective conjunction. Try to avoid using 'and' more than once in a sentence. "Sex and drugs and rock and roll" may be all very well as a song lyric, but in written English, "sex, drugs and rock 'n' roll" is preferable. Avoid using 'and' to connect series of clauses, as "She rushed in from work and took her coat off and listened to the answering machine and made herself a cup of tea and sat down and wept." And finally, don't listen to pedants who maintain that it is bad English to begin a sentence with 'and.' Respectable authors have done this for more than a thousand years, using the initial 'and' to facilitate narrative – "And then there was the one about … " or to express the archness of a question – "And who do you think you are?" – or simply to give emphasis – "And how!"

Andalusia English rendering of the name of the southernmost province of Spain, known locally as Andalucia.

androgynous Buzz word describing a person of ambiguous sexuality. Greek *andros* (man) and *gune* (woman).

Andromeda

Andromeda   Heroine of Greek mythology gave her name to a galaxy that is the nearest to our own, and at 2.2 million light years distant, the furthest object in the night sky visible to the naked eye.

anecdote   A short recounting of an event. In law, witness testimony to a court may be dismissed as "anecdotal" – hearsay – rather than material evidence. In medical research, "anecdotal" evidence of the efficacy of a treatment is usually considered of less value than trial results in which some patients with a particular illness are given a drug, others are given a placebo, and the results compared later. Greek *anekdota* (items unpublished).

Anglo-Saxon   The Germanic language used in the British Isles from the fifth century AD by the English Saxons – who migrated to England from Saxony. Now, the description Anglo-Saxon is frequently used to assert a sort of indigenous Britishness in some sections of the population, with an implied racial superiority over those descended from later arrivals, such as the Vikings, the Normans, various refugees – Huguenots, Jews – and, more recently, immigrants from the former British Empire as well as today's 'asylum seekers.' Anglo-Saxon is the source of many of the most-used words in the English language, including many of the obscenities. Thus, phrases such as 'an Anglo-Saxon outburst' or 'a torrent of Anglo-Saxon' are common euphemisms (*qv*) for the use of bad language.

annal   Strictly speaking, a record of one year's events, but now loosely used to mean any defined strand in history, as 'the annals of the de Courcy dynasty.' From Latin *annus* (year). Note the double 'n.' Anal means of the anus, with metaphoric inferences pertaining to narrow-mindedness.

annex   Verb meaning to seize land by conquest. Do not confuse spelling with annexe – a type of extension to a building.

annexe   see annex.

annul   To declare or make invalid. Takes two ls in annulled and annulling but one in annulment.

annotation   Notes added to explain details of text or sources of research in text, either as footnotes on the respective page or in an appendix.

anodyne   From a word that once meant a pain-relieving preparation, this new adjective purports to mean dull or contrived to give no offence. Greek *anodonus* (painless).

anonymous   Unidentified by name, as an anonymous author. Greek *anonumos* (nameless).

anorak   Innuit word for a hooded jacket (note spelling is not 'anorack') has entered 21st century English as a pleasing metaphor for the type of anorak-wearer who enjoys minority pursuits such as real-ale drinking and train spotting.

anptyxis   Adding an extra vowel between consonants for emphasis, as "she went thataway."

antagonist   In a play or novel the antagonist is the principal character in opposition to the hero (the protagonist).

ante-   Prefix denoting 'before.' Most words starting with it are spelled as one – antecedent, antediluvian, antenatal – but exceptions include ante-bellum (in the time before the war) and ante-post (of horse-race betting before runners' numbers are posted). The 'ante' in a poker game is a fixed stake pledged before the cards are dealt and the word is now in metaphorical use for sums of money risked, as in 'competition raises the ante.' Beware confusion with prefix 'anti-.' Latin *ante* (before).

antediluvian   Fancy word for outdated or old-fashioned. It means 'before the Flood' and is frequently misspelled.

anthology   A collection of literary works, usually poetry, essays or short stories. The most famous of verse anthologies, Francis Palgrave's *Golden Treasury* of 1861 established the genre once and for all.

anthropo-   Prefix denoting reference to mankind. An anthropoid is a man-like creature, an anthropologist is a student of mankind and anthropomorphism is the attribution of human characteristics to pagan gods, animals or, latterly, any kind of object. Greek *anthropos* (man).

anti-

anti-   Prefix denoting 'against.' Most words starting with it are spelled as one – anticlimax, antidote, antisocial – but hyphenated exceptions include anti-hero (in fiction), anti-lock (brakes), anti-personnel (weapon) and anti-semitic. Beware confusion with prefix 'ante-.' Greek *anti* (against).

anticlimax   In literature, the dwindling of an exciting narrative to an unexpectedly disappointing conclusion. Mostly a device of comic writing – but also an unwitting feature of much bad writing, especially for television.

anti-hero   In literature, the central character of a story or play notable for his or her lack of the usual virtues of courage, loyalty, forbearance etc, but who nevertheless elicits sympathy on the narrative road to disaster (or, occasionally, unexpected success). The literature of the 21st century has yet to produce an anti-hero with lasting merit, but enduring popular anti-heroes of the 20th century include Yossarian in Joseph Heller's Second World War epic *Catch 22*, and the revived villain Harry Flashman, purloined from Thomas Hughes's *Tom Brown's Schooldays* for the series of *Flashman* stories by George Macdonald Fraser.

Antipodes   Australia and New Zealand, as described from the northern hemisphere. The word merely means any place that is diametrically opposite to another. Australians and New Zealanders could quite legitimately refer to their constitutional begetter, Great Britain, as the Antipodes, but gallantly refrain from doing so. Greek *antipodes* (having the feet opposite).

antiphrasis   Figure of speech in which a word is used to convey the opposite of its customary meaning, as in the ironic use of 'beautiful' to describe a hideous scene. Greek *antiphrasis* (expressed as opposite).

antipophora   Figure of speech in which a speaker poses a question then answers it himself, as "am I a fool? Of course I am." Greek antipophora (against answer).

antithesis   In literature, a character, idea or situation that is the diametric opposite of another. Greek *antitithemi* (set against).

antonomasia   In linguistics, the use of a real or imaginary individual's name to typify a person or a mode of behaviour, as "he's a right little Hitler" or "the greed of Shylock." Greek *antonomazo* (name instead).

antonym   A word that means the opposite of another, as bad is the antonym of good. From French.

antsy   Recent word for anxious or irritable. Adapted from phrase 'ants in your pants.'

any more   This phrase, as in 'he doesn't love me any more,' is correctly written as two words. The word 'anymore' is common enough in written English, but strictly speaking does not exist.

Apartheid   Specifically, the officially sanctioned system under which racial groups were segregated in South Africa from 1948 to 1991. Now, with a lower case initial, any forced division between groups. Afrikaans for 'separateness.'

aphorism   A pithy statement that becomes idiomatic in the language. Invented by ancient Greek physician Hippocrates (*c.*460–377BC) whose celebrated work *Aphorisms* begins with the eternal motto "Life is short. Art is lasting."

Apocalypse   The end of the world, as described in Revelation, the concluding book of the Bible. Now, written with a lower case initial, any major catastrophe. Greek *apokaluptein* (to reveal).

apocope   In linguistics, the omission of the end of a word, as 'loadsamoney' cuts the 'f' from 'of.'

apocryphal   Originally, from the Apocrypha – the writings excluded from edited versions of the Christian Scriptures. Thus, later, a narrative of doubtful origin or truthfulness, even though widely believed.

apologist   Not someone who apologises, but one who argues in favour of a cause that might be widely despised, as 'an apologist for Robert Mugabe's land-grab campaign.'

apologue   Not an apology but a moral fable, particularly one in which the characters are animals. George Orwell's novel ridiculing the tenets of communism, *Animal Farm* (1945), is an apologue.

apophthegm A proclaimed motto or maxim, as 'love conquers all.' Greek *apophthengesthai* (to speak out).

aporia An irreparable breakdown in the logic of an argument. Greek *aporos* (impassable).

apostrophe Punctuation mark denoting possession or abbreviation. Its misuse is one of the most common failings in written English, and yet the rules for its correct use are simple. First, be aware that apostrophes are always used as device of brevity. "My father's house" is the modern, shortened English for what would once have been "the house of my father." And "that's life" is the modern, shortened English for what would once have been "that is life." These two uses summarise the entire function of the apostrophe.

There remains the little problem of where the apostrophe goes according to single and plural possessive use. But again, it's simple. If the possessor is single, as in "the girl's hat" the apostrophe is placed before the 's.' If the possessor is plural, as in "the girls' school" the apostrophe goes after the 's' because it is, in effect, abbreviating what would otherwise be "the girls's school." Remember that collective words, such as children, crowd and people, are singular, so in the possessive are written as "the children's party", "the crowd's favourite", "the people's friend" and so on.

Where the word ends in 's' there is a tendency among some writers to shorten the possessive form, as in "Prince Charles' horse" instead of "Prince Charles's horse." But there is no reason to break the basic rule simply for words ending in 's.' It makes no more sense to say "Charles' horse" than it would to say "Camilla' horse." Use the apostrophe with consistency, and much dithering over correctness will be saved. And ignore the ancient convention that Jesus takes a unique possessive, as in "Jesus' disciples." Not even the son of God should be made, or surely would demand to be made, an exception to a very sensible rule.

One more convention concerns the apostrophe in sequence. Do you write "Adam and Eve's expulsion from the Garden of Eden" or "Adam's and Eve's expulsion … "? No firm rule here, but where the two or more subjects form a familiar whole – as Adam and Eve do – use the apostrophe only on the last possessive noun. Where the two or more subjects are dissociated, use the apostrophe each time, as in "it was America's, and the world's, worst disaster."

In the 21st century, the erosion of the apostrophe will no doubt continue. In fairness, it was introduced into English as an abbreviation as recently as the 16th century, and as a possessive indicator in the 18th, so as a form of punctuation it is hardly founded in antiquity. Presumably for graphic simplicity, the names of many public organisations have dispensed with the apostrophe. Examples are Diners Club (solving the problem of whether to call it Diner's or Diners') and Reuters (originally Reuter's, after founder Paul Julius Reuter).

Possessive pronouns do not take the apostrophe, because they are possessive words in their own right. Nevertheless, it is common to see "it's" or even "its' " mistakenly written into a phrase intended to say something like "the animal broke free from its tether" and even "hers' " and "theirs.' " Avoid!

appal Note the single 'l,' but spellings appalled and appalling.

appendix Additional matter to the general text of a book or document. Dictionaries give two plural forms, appendices and appendixes. Latin *appendare* (to hang on).

appraise and **apprise** Appraise means to evaluate, as a dealer appraises a painting. Apprise means to inform, as the dealer apprises his client of the painting's value.

APR On advertisements for 'financial services' – money lending – the Annual Percentage Rate of interest chargeable. This must be stated on loan offers according to UK law.

aqu- All words beginning with this prefix refer either to water or to eagles, eg aquarium, aqueduct and aquiline. All other English words with the prefix sound 'akwa' are spelled acqu-, acquire, acquit etc.

Arabic numerals The figures used in western writing – 1, 2, 3 etc – are Arabic, as distinct from Roman I, II, III etc.

arc and **ark**   An arc is a curve (from Latin *arcus*, a bow) and an ark is a ship, as in Noah's rescue vessel from the Old Testament (from Latin *arca*, a chest).

arch-   This prefix denotes a chief or leader, as in archbishop, architect, arch-fiend. Greek *arkhos* (chief).

archaeology   Note spelling. Omitting the second 'a' is only American English.

archaic   In language, a word or phrase considered long out of use.

archetype   An unmistakably typical example, as "Saddam Hussein is an archetype of modern tyranny." Some dictionaries give the adjectival form archetypical, but archetypal is usual.

architectural styles   The British custom of naming the style of buildings after the reigning monarch (Elizabethan, Jacobean, Victorian) or royal line (Tudor, Georgian) of the time in which they are assumed to have been built originated with the statesman and popular historian Thomas Babington Macaulay (1800–59). It is a decorous way of referring to architectural styles, but can frequently prove chronologically wide of the mark. 'Victorian' tends to be applied to anything built in the 19th century in spite of the fact that Queen Victoria's reign began more than a third of the way through it, in 1837.

ard   Lost word for the first non-lethal implement wielded by early mankind. It was a heavy pointed stick used to scratch and disturb the soil – the forerunner of the plough.

argot   Slang of a particular group, as in the argot of jazz enthusiasts. French *argot*.

argument   Two distinct meanings: A heated exchange of views, and a case presented for judgement. Latin *arguere*, meaning both to accuse and to prove.

ark   See arc.

-arium   Words with this suffix denote some kind of room or container, as in solarium and aquarium. From Latin *caldarium* (hot room), *frigidarium* (cold room) etc.

armageddon Buzz word for a catastrophe is lifted from the last book of the New Testament, *Revelation*. The biblical event was the final conflict between heaven and hell. Hebrew *har megiddon* (hill of Megiddo).

Army When referring to the regular army of your own nation, use an initial capital, as in "my brother has just joined the Army." The same applies to other armed forces, notably the Navy and Air Force.

around and **round** As a preposition, among the meanings of 'around' are being alive or in the vicinity, as in "she's still around." In this sense, the preposition 'round' should not be used. In the other sense, on all sides of, as in "we're going (a)round the world," both are now commonly used, but 'around' is still identifiably an American usage, while 'round' is more identified with British English.

artefact or **artifact** Both spellings are used, but try to be consistent.

artiste Only a musical stage or circus performer takes the 'e.'

as vs **like** Make it a rule never to substitute as with like. 'Do as I do' is correct. 'Do like I do' is an affront, and unnecessary.

asinine Behaving like an ass. Note only one 's.' From Latin *asinus* (ass).

ask New noun, as in "a big ask" to denote a major challenge.

assassin Note spelling. The word derives from Arabic *hashshashin* (hashish-user), the name given to drug-deranged Muslim killers at the time of the Crusades, from the 11th century.

assonance In writing, especially poetry and song lyrics, a resemblance between words used to form a loose rhyme, as in Sir Cliff Richard's immortal lyric "Christmas time, mistletoe and wine, Children singing Christian rhyme."

assurance The British insurance industry, curiously, sells 'assurance' rather than insurance on lives.

asterisk Star mark (*) in text indicating a note elsewhere. Not to be confused with Asterix, the Gaul.

asthma

asthma Note spelling. The word is Greek, describing an affliction as well known in the time of the physician Hippocrates (*c.*460–377BC) as it is today.

astrology and **astronomy** Astrology is the ancient study of the stars and planets in the context of their movements' influence on the human and natural world. Astronomy is the study of space.

asyndeton Leaving out the conjunction in a phrase for dramatic effect, as in "I came, I saw, I conquered." Greek *a* (not) and *sundetos* (tied together) – the same root as 'asunder.'

atavistic Buzz word correctly means primitive, as in a reversion to the customs or practices of long ago, as in "the understandably atavistic behaviour of a lone man shipwrecked on a desert island." Latin *atavus* (forefather).

aubade A poem or piece of music on a theme connected to dawn. Spanish *alba* (dawn).

auger and **augur** An auger is a drilling tool and an augur a soothsayer in ancient Rome. The verb to augur means to foretell as, "today's performance augurs well for the rest of the season."

Augustan Age High-falluting name for an early 18th-century movement in English literature. Writers such as Addison, Pope and Swift aspired to the liberalism, reason, patriotism and wit of the Roman writers of the Augustan age (27BC to 14AD).

Aunt Sally Outdated figurative term for a person or thing held up as an object for abuse. Originally, an Aunt Sally was a grotesque, pipe-smoking model figure erected in fairgrounds as a target for ball-throwing contestants in pursuit of a prize for the first missile to succeed in breaking off the pipe.

author Writer of books, articles or any other documentary work. The word is not exclusive to fiction or drama.

auto- Words with this prefix indicate self, as an autodidact is a self-taught person, an automatic device is self-activating and an autocrat is someone ruling on their own. Greek *autos* (self).

autobiography Book or story of the author's own life.

auxiliary verb   In grammar, a verb that is auxiliary in the sense that it forms the mood, tense or voice of another verb. There are three auxiliary verbs: to be, to have and to do, as in "I may be going abroad tomorrow," etc. See also modal verbs.

avant-garde   In the arts, including literature, work that is new and experimental. French for advance guard, as in an army.

B

back-formation   A new word formed from an existing one, although appearing as if it should have come first, as in televise from original television and emote from original emotion.

back slang   Words created by reversing others, usually for comic effect, as Shakespeare the Drab (from the Bard) and yob from boy.

bail and **bale**   Bail has several meanings, the three most used being (1) the money paid to secure the release of a prisoner (and thus also to bail someone out of any kind of financial trouble), (2) a section of wood that rests on top of cricket stumps and (3) as a verb, to scoop water out of a boat to prevent it sinking. Bale has two principal meanings, (1) a bundle of material, such as straw or fabric and (2) as a verb, to escape a doomed aircraft, as in to bale out. One complication is that 'bail out' is also commonly used to describe the airborne exit, and dictionaries studiously avoid saying it is incorrect to do so.

bait and **bate**   To bait is to entice, as by luring fish with a bait on a hook and line. To bait is also to tease or torment. There is no verb to bate – just the slang term meaning a fit of bad temper, as in "there's no need to get into such a bate about it."

bale   See bail.

ballad   Originally a rendition of a traditional legend in the form of a song or verse. Now as likely to describe any sentimental popular song. Provençal *balada* (a dancing song).

balmy and **barmy**   Balmy (as in 'a balmy night') means soothing, as in the effect of applying a balm – a healing ointment. Beware confusion with 'barmy,' British English slang for crazy.

baluster   A stair-rail support (often in a balustrade). Note spelling, with a single 'l.'

banister   A stair rail. Note spelling, with a single 'n.' Recent dictionaries say 'also bannister' but only because the word has been so long misspelt – largely thanks to the fame of Sir Roger

Bannister, the first man to run a mile in under four minutes, in 1954. But don't run with the crowd, spell banister correctly.

Bar When referring to the body and profession of barristers-at-law, as in the phrase "called to the Bar" it is customary but not compulsory to use the initial capital.

bard A poet. Referring to England's William Shakespeare and Scotland's Robert Burns, it is still customary to use the initial capital when describing each as his country's Bard, in the sense of national poet. Welsh *bardd* from Celtic.

baroque The ornate style of 17th- and 18th-century European art extended beyond architecture and design into music and literature. Consequently, critics today might well describe the over-elaborate language of some writers, in the present and recent past as well as of the period itself, as 'baroque.' Mostly, though, the term will be used simply to ridicule the subject matter. Portuguese *barroco*.

basically In conversation, this is usually just a spacer, as in "Basically, he's a complete swine." Besides use in reported speech, avoid in written work.

bate See bait.

bathos In literature, a sudden shift from a sublime theme to a ridiculous one. Greek *bathos* (depth).

batty Recent synonym for gay, in sense of homosexual.

baulk In the sense of to refuse, as in "he baulked at committing a crime" use the complete word. Balk is American English.

BBC English The Corporation has long maintained a rigorous style-book on the use of English. There is a 'Pronunciation Unit' to ensure consistency in broadcasts, and in 1992 the first *BBC English Dictionary* was published, featuring "the English used by the BBC World Service."

beguile This picturesque verb has two distinct meanings. One is to charm, perhaps to the point of deluding, as "he beguiled her into trusting him." The other is to while away, as "she beguiled the hours with reverie."

bellwether

bellwether The leading sheep in a flock, and thus an indicator of a mood or movement. Note spelling.

berth A tying-up place for a ship, or sleeping quarters on board. Do not confuse with birth.

bevy A group, usually of people, as 'a bevy of beauties.' Beware confusion with 'bevvy' – Northern English and Scottish slang for a strong drink.

biannual and **biennial** Biannual means twice a year. Biennial means every other year.

bibliography A list of the published sources consulted for any written work. Greek *biblio* (book) and *graphia* (writing).

billion Strictly speaking an American billion is a thousand million, and a British billion is a million million. But when British newspapers and broadcasters refer to the world's population being six billion, they nevertheless mean six thousand million. In the 21st century, the American billion holds sway.

binge Now a verb, from the noun meaning excessive eating, drinking or spending. In the participle form, use bingeing, not binging.

biography The story of an individual life – not written by the author. See also autobiography.

birth See berth.

black In the 21st century, it is probably as acceptable to describe one person as black as it is to describe another as white.

black comedy A narrative in which comedy and tragedy intermingle. The ancient meaning of 'comedy' is not a funny story, but one which resolves in a successful outcome for the hero, as distinct from a tragic ending. This defines black comedy as well, with the tale ending in the main character's triumph over adversity.

blank verse Poetry that does not rhyme. It is not a modern aberration, in spite of what is said by vociferous critics of some contemporary poetry. William Shakespeare and John Milton, among the two greatest poets in the English language, both wrote extensively in blank verse.

blend   A new word formed by joining two existing words, as 'docudrama' or 'glitterati.' See also portmanteau words.

bling-bling   Recent onomatopoeic term for young person wearing an excess of jewellery, and subsequently anyone displaying ostentatious wealth. Originally associated with rap and hip-hop culture. Now commonly shortened to bling.

bloc   Originally French, it was much used in the 20th century for strategic groupings of federated or allied nations or interested parties, such as the Soviet bloc. But the distinct spelling, even in this sense, is gradually waning in favour of block.

blond or **blonde**   Strictly speaking, the word only takes the 'e' when used to describe the woman as a person rather than her fair hair in particular. So, a woman might be a blonde, but her hair is blond. Fair boys and men are blond, and so is their fair hair. French.

blue sky thinking   A 21st-century idiom roughly equating to 'seeing with a fresh eye' and quoted by political spin doctors as a quality sought in nominees for government advisory posts. An example was the 2001 appointment of former BBC chief Lord Birt to advise on the long-term future of Britain's troubled railway network. When Opposition MPs objected that Birt had no knowledge of railways, government spokesmen were able to reply that this was exactly what qualified him. He would bring blue sky thinking to the task.

bluestocking   Until well into the last century, bluestocking was a patronising word for a female intellectual – a woman dedicating herself to matters of the mind at the expense of her 'duties' as wife, mother and homemaker. But in the 21st century, to call a woman a bluestocking is to compliment her. The original bluestockings were a tiny minority of women in the mid-18th century, taking their name from the colour of hosiery they were reputed to wear, who managed against the odds to enter higher education, science and the arts. Today, with women taking rather more than half of the places at universities and in the professions, a contemporary bluestocking tends to be a woman of outstanding intellect, even by female standards.

boatswain Long pronounced 'bosun' the word for a ship's officer is now more commonly spelled this way, too. Other variations bo'sun and bo's'n are effectively extinct.

BOGOF Sounds like an impolite injunction of dismissal, but it is a current marketing acronym for 'Buy One Get One Free.'

bollocks An expletive that has, regrettably, survived intact into the 21st century. The dictionaries are pretty much in agreement that it means 'balls' – once as in testicles, but now as in 'rubbish.' Only 50 years ago, it was commonly pronounced 'ballocks.' See also dog's bollocks.

book titles When typing work on a word processor, it is good practice to italicise book titles, as "Tolstoy's novel *War and Peace* gives uncanny signs of impending revolution." In handwriting, clarify reference to titles by using single quote marks, as "Tolstoy's novel 'War and Peace' … See also publication titles.

born and **borne** A baby is born, and the pain of its birth is borne by the mother. Both words are past participles of the verb to bear. Use borne for all occasions except in the sense of a baby being born.

botanical names The species-identifying Latin names of plants should be written with an initial capital for the genus and lower case for the species, as in *Quercus robur* for English oak. Use italics.

bowdlerise An eponym (*qv*) meaning to edit a book so insensitively and censoriously that the work is ruined. After Thomas Bowdler (1754–1825) notorious for his expurgated edition of the works of William Shakespeare.

breach and **breech** A breach is a break, act of breaking or opening, as in 'a breach of the peace' or 'the cavalry poured through the breach in the enemy's line.' A breech is the rear portion of a gun barrel or a garment resembling trousers (now always pluralized to breeches). A breech birth is so called, because the baby's backside emerges first.

breath and **breathe** Breath is the noun, as in 'he could scarcely draw breath.' Breathe is the verb, as in 'he could scarcely breathe.'

Brit Americans may call the British Brits, but we should not describe ourselves as such. A brit, as mentioned as long ago as 1755 by Dr Johnson in his *Dictionary*, is a kind of fish.

Britain Synonymous with the United Kingdom, namely England, Scotland, Wales and Northern Ireland. Strictly speaking, Great Britain encompasses only the mainland and thus excludes Northern Ireland.

British Isles All of the United Kingdom and – geographically rather than politically – the entire island of Ireland.

Briton Any member of the population of Britain. The 'ancient Britons' were members of the Brythonic Celtic tribes – Breton, Cornish and Welsh – who preceded the Romans in Britain.

Brontë As in the 19th-century novelists Anne, Charlotte and Emily, always write with the diaeresis (ë).

Brownsigner New slang for a young person in metropolitan society who seeks liaisons with wealthy, landed men or women whose ancestral country homes are open to the public, and signposted with brown tourist landmark signs from surrounding roads.

B2B Business to business. Internet term for online commercial information or transaction between businesses.

B2C Business to consumer/customer. Internet term for online information or selling direct to consumers.

bucolic Oft-misused word means pastoral – as in rural – as, "they dreamed of quitting London to begin a bucolic life in Somerset.' Greek *boukolos* (herdsman).

bugger Once a very offensive word understood to mean a sodomite, this has evolved almost to a term of affection, as in "he's a well-meaning old bugger." The word's origin is correspondingly mild, being a Middle English corruption of Bulgarian, synonymous with a member of Bulgaria's Orthodox church and thus, in the view of the Catholic church, a heretic.

bureau In the plural, use bureaux, as this is a French word.

burger and **burgher** A burger is a meat patty. A burgher is a citizen of a borough.

burglar

burglar A criminal who enters a premises with intent to steal. Until a UK legal redefinition of 1969, burglary could only be committed by night – as distinct from daylight robbery. Now, a building is burgled and a person is robbed, whatever the time of day.

burlesque A book or play founded in absurdity. In the US, a variety show incorporating a striptease. Italian *burlesco*.

Bushisms The 21st century began with a new President of the United States, George W Bush Jnr. Already notorious for his nonsensical utterances, he did not let his tenure of the highest office break him of the habit. Following are a few of the most-quoted of his solecisms (*qv*):

"Oftentimes our teachers come out of their pocketbooks to meet the supply needs of students."

"It isn't pollution that's harming the environment. It's the impurities in our air and water that are doing it."

"The vast majority of our imports come from outside the country."

"Verbosity leads to unclear, inarticulate things."

"The trouble with the French is they don't have a word for entrepreneur."

"I know how hard it is to put food on your family."

businessman One word, and likewise for businesswoman. Eschew businessperson(s).

but The main adversative conjunction, and the one much to be preferred over the unwieldy 'however.' The convention that it is incorrect to begin a sentence with 'But' has, happily, failed to make it into the 21st century. Use the introductive conjunction as an aid to keeping sentences short. Thus, 'She had told him she loved him only the day before. But here she was already, claiming it had been a joke.'

by and **bye** Only in the default cricket score and in goodbye/bye bye does 'by' exclusively take an 'e.' Bye-law and by-law are both equally common spellings now.

Byron, George Gordon, 6th Baron Lord Byron (1788–1824) was a fecund neologist (inventor of words) as well as an immortal poet and inveterate cad. Words he brought into the English language include the appropriately languid terms *blasé* and *bored*.

Byzantine It refers to ancient Byzantium, the empire of AD 395 to 1453 of the sacred city of Constantinople, now the Istanbul of modern Turkey. As well as describing the history, architecture and practices of the empire, Byzantine has come to denote administrations or hierarchies that are unwieldy or rigid, as in 'the Byzantine bureaucracy of Italian regional government.' Always use the initial capital.

C

cacao and **cocoa** Cacao is the tree from whose seed pods cocoa is extracted to make chocolate. See also coca.

caddie and **caddy** A caddie is a golfer's assistant. A caddy is a container for tea leaves.

Caesarean Not 'Caesarian.' Lower case initial is now more common, but worth avoiding.

café Write with the accent.

callous and **callus** Callous is an adjective meaning hard-hearted. A callus is a thickened expanse of skin, especially on hands or feet.

cannon and **canon** A cannon is a large gun or a collision between balls in billiards. A canon is a clergyman, a division of ecclesiastical law or a body of work.

cant Cant is empty, pious talk. Can't is a contraction of 'can not,' synonymous with cannot. Kant is the name of one of the greatest figures in western philosophy, Germany's Immanuel Kant (1724–1804).

canvas and **canvass** Canvas is sailcloth. To canvass is to solicit opinions or votes.

capital Even in 'the capital' to denote London, there is no need to use an initial capital. But beware reference to the building that houses the US Congress in Washington, DC, the Capitol.

capital and **corporal** Beware confusing capital and corporal in law. A 'capital offence' is a crime punishable by death. A 'corporal punishment' is one in which pain is inflicted on the body.

capital letters A capital is always used for the first letter of a sentence. It is a universal rule. But the same cannot be said for the capitalization of names or 'proper' nouns. Style varies wildly between – and even within – publications such as national newspapers and magazines. Apply commonsense rules. All names of people and places – Peter Cook, Paraguay, Piccadilly Circus –

take capitals. All titles of specific works of art – *Citizen Kane*, the *Mona Lisa*, Beethoven's Fifth Symphony, *Anna Karenina* – take a capital. Languages and nationalities – English, the French – take capitals. Institutions – the Houses of Parliament, the White House, the Anglican Church – take capitals. Days, months and formally defined periods of history – Monday, February, the Middle Ages – take capitals. Capitalize compass points where they refer to a formally recognised region, as in the North or the South East (for example of England). Capitalize the Earth, the Moon, the Sun and the Solar System.

Words deriving from proper names usually take a capital – as Christian from Christ and Marxist from Marx. But some such words, known as eponyms, have come into everyday use and no longer take a capital. See entry for eponyms. Trademarked words should take capitals – Adidas, Mercedes, Smarties – unless, of course, the logo uses lower case, as in fcuk.

Capital letters are used for titles, but not for job descriptions other than formal or official ones such as the Chancellor of the Exchequer, the US President etc. For an office holder in a company, write: "Managing Director Sheila Smith said … " but "Sheila Smith, the managing director, said … "

Even in the 21st century it is still customary to capitalize the deity: Allah, the Almighty, God. But capitalizing possessive references, such as "God in His wisdom" is now falling out of use. But if quoting direct from scripture or texts such as the *Book of Common Prayer*, follow the form as printed, as in "Hallowed be thy Name."

A recent arrival is the 'medial' capital, as used in the BBC TV soap opera *EastEnders*. Odd though the contrivance may look, the style of the title should be followed.

Capitol   See capital.

carat and **caret**   A carat is a gold-purity measure. A caret is an insert mark used in manual text correction.

carcase   Meaning a dead body or, more recently, a framework, this used to have the common alternative spelling carcass. Stick to carcase now.

caricature   In literature, a distorted parody, as "the head teacher was the victim of a cruel caricature in the school magazine." Also a verb, as in "he was cruelly caricatured." Italian *caricatura*.

Caroline   Historians have a tendency to use this word to describe English periods defined by the reigns of kings Charles I (1625–49) and Charles II (1660-85). 'Carolean' is also used. From Latin *Carolus*, the origin of the modern name Charles.

case   In Latin, nouns have six cases. They are nominative, vocative, accusative, genitive, dative and ablative. These respective cases greatly influenced the development of English until the Norman Conquest of 1066, but have now all-but disappeared, leaving three residual cases – subjective, objective and possessive. They are now evident only in pronouns, as in (respectively) I, me, my; he, him, his; we, us, our etc.

In typography, the case of letters is either lower, as in small letters, or upper, as in capitals.

cata-   Words with this prefix often denote some sort of negative or reverse. In its original Greek a catastrophe means a reversal of fortune. Greek *kata* (back or down).

catachresis   Inappropriate use of a word or phrase, usually deliberately in a contrived mixed metaphor (*qv*), as in, 'back to back, they faced each other … drew their swords and shot each other.' Greek *katachresis* (misuse).

catalyst   Beware this weasel word. It is a term from chemistry to describe a substance that alters the rate of reaction with other chemicals but does not itself undergo any permanent change in the process. It is widely used in metaphor to suggest any agent of change, but is accurately applied only when the catalyst in question is specifically immune from the effects of the process it influences.

catharsis   Buzz word means a process of purification often through a traumatic experience, as 'the loss of her mother was a catharsis.' Greek *katharos* (pure).

Catholic   When describing the Roman church, its customs and beliefs, or one of its members, always write Catholic with an initial capital. Written as catholic, the word has a very different modern meaning – embracing a wide variety of beliefs, tastes or things. With or without the initial capital, the word derives from Greek *katholikos* (universal).

caulk   The verb meaning to make a barrel or boat hull watertight by pressing tarred material between staves or boards should be spelled with the 'u' because the alternative spelling, calk, given in dictionaries has other distinct meanings.

Cavalier   A member of the Royalist faction in the English Civil Wars of the 1640s and, more loosely – and without the initial capital – an adjective denoting off-hand or haughty behaviour, as "he was infuriated to be treated in such a cavalier manner."

caviar   The old form 'caviare' has not made it into the 21st century.

-ceed   This suffix completes only three words in English: exceed, proceed and succeed. The suffix -cede is much the more common, as in accede, concede, intercede, precede, recede etc.

Celsius   Now commonly used as an alternative to centigrade in the temperature scale. Write with an initial capital, as it is the name of Anders Celsius (1701–44) who devised the first centigrade thermometer.

censer and **censor**   A censer is an incense burner. A censor is an official who checks written, filmed or broadcast material for acceptability in accordance with varying criteria including decency, legality and political correctness.

centigrade   The 21st century has finally ushered in the decimal temperature scale for weather reporting in the United Kingdom. Write the generic centigrade without an initial capital, but its alternative, Celsius (*qv*) with one.

century   With a capital 'c'? It is no more necessary to use the initial capital in '19th century' than it is in 'at the end of the century.' Bear in mind the newspaper sub-editor's rule: only use initial capitals when you have to.

chairman   The term has survived into the 21st century, along with the more recent chairwoman. Either is surely preferable to the horribly contrived chairperson – or chair.

Chambers Dictionary

Chambers Dictionary William and Robert Chambers were publishers in Edinburgh of a weekly magazine, *Chambers's Journal*. Launched in 1832, its success enabled the brothers to extend into reference book publishing, first with their *Cyclopaedia of English Literature* in 1844. The first edition of the *Chambers English Dictionary* appeared in 1872, and has been widely regarded as a dependable, scholarly and timely lexicon with every edition published since.

champagne Write the word describing the famed sparkling wine without an initial capital. In France, *le champagne* (the wine) comes from *La Champagne* (the region).

character As an element in fiction and drama, character – as distinct from plot and narrative – describes the type and nature of people depicted.

characters In typography, the letters and punctuation that make up words and phrases. 'Crash!' has eight characters (three of them punctuation marks).

charisma Enduring buzz word once meant a talent conferred on a mortal by a deity, but the sense has long since migrated to little more than the kind of charm that inspires devotion in followers. Greek *kharis* (grace).

chattel A portable possession. Note spelling.

chav Current pejorative slang for a young person identified as working class and undereducated by their choice of cheap sportswear. See also pikey. The term, which may be contracted from 'Chatham vandals' – gangs of youths said to plague the town of Chatham, east of London – has largely displaced the former gender-specific kev and sharon.

cheers Once a toast, equivalent to 'good health' this word has acquired equivalence with several other words and phrases, including 'thank you' and 'goodbye.' The word derives via French from Latin *cara* (face).

chestnut A species of nut-bearing tree, but also a corny old joke or tired cliché.

chiasmus Figure of speech with reversing structures in successive phrases, as in 'the Sabbath was made for man, not man for the Sabbath' and 'you should eat to live, not live to eat.' Greek *chiasma* (a cross-shaped mark).

chick-lit Derogatory term for popular fiction written by young women for an audience of young women. Avoid.

chivvy Write with the double 'v.' The word, meaning to instruct repeatedly, is said to derive from a hunting cry used long ago in the Scottish border country.

chord and **cord** A chord is a harmonic group of notes in music. A cord is a connective rope, as in rip cord or spinal cord.

chorus In ancient Greece, the chorus (originally meaning dance) was a group of performers at a religious festival. As drama grew out of these rites, the chorus gradually assumed the role of commentator on the action. By the time of Shakespeare, the chorus was an individual actor in the role of commentator and continuity announcer as plays progressed – a function now familiar in the voiceovers often written into TV and film drama.

Christian Use the capital C.

Christian name For given names – the John in John Smith – this is in danger of becoming politically incorrect in the multicultural context. First name, forename and given name are the usual substitutes.

chronic It means lingering and long-lasting, as in chronic medical conditions. Greek *chronos* (time).

chronicle A record of events as they have occurred over time. Greek *chronos* (time).

chronological In order of occurrence. To relate events in chronological order is to arrange them in time and/or date order. Greek *chronos* (time).

cinquain In poetry, a verse of five lines.

cinque ports Persistent medieval reference to five English towns granted trading privileges. They are Dover, Hastings, Hythe, Romney and Sandwich.

cite and **site**   To cite is to give as an example, as, "he cited his own experiences of train travel to illustrate the dire state of the railway system." To site is to locate or position, as "the factory was sited close to the motorway."

classic   As an adjective, it means something of recognised quality that has stood the test of time, as in 'a classic car.' It can also mean characteristic or typical, as 'classic symptoms of the disease.' As a noun, familiar senses are a book or even a sports event described admiringly as 'a classic.'

Classical   It is helpful, when referring specifically to the period of history dominated by ancient Greece and Rome, to capitalise the word Classical, as in the Classical World. This gives separation from 'classical' as in music or other distinct senses.

classical allusion   Once upon a time, storytellers filled their writings with allusions – references – to characters from the mythologies of ancient Greece and Rome. A hero with an 'Achilles heel' was a strong man, but with a fatal weakness, as in the one vulnerable spot on the body of the Greek hero of Troy, Achilles. The story goes that as a baby he was dipped by his mother in the river Styx to make him immune to injury. But the heel she held him by was untouched by the water. Many classical allusions, however, are less familiar than this one and their use has gradually disappeared from literature as the study of the old mythologies – among writers as well as readers – has waned. Nevertheless, a little knowledge of classical allusion can still be a useful asset to readers and writers today. After all, the names of the planets in our solar system – and many of the stars and galaxies beyond – come from the myths, as do countless names from the arts and commerce. Following are a few of the most common references.

Adonis   Now, a very handsome young man. In Greek myth, a young man adored by the goddess Aphrodite.

Aegis   The shield of Jupiter, and thus now used in the context of protection, as in "under the aegis of the Crown."

Aeneas   Son of Anchises and Aphrodite who fled Troy and, as told in Virgil's *Aeneid*, journeyed to pre-Roman Italy.

Agamemnon   Ruler of Argos who led the Greek expedition against Troy. On his return, he was murdered by his wife, Clytemnaestra.

Ajax   Warrior prince of Salamis who sailed with 12 ships to Troy. Second in bravery only to Achilles, he died after losing the contest for Achilles's armour to Odysseus.

Andromeda   Princess of Aethiopia whose mother, Cassiopeia, boasted was more beautiful than the sea nymphs. This angered Poseidon, who sent a sea monster to terrorise the kingdom. The creature could only be placated, according to an oracle, if Andromeda were given up to it, and her father was compelled to chain her to a rock on the seashore as a sacrifice. But she was rescued by Perseus, who in some versions of the myth killed the monster by showing it the severed head of the Medusa. Any living thing that looked on the head was turned to stone. In astronomy, the galaxy of Andromeda is the nearest to Earth, and the only one visible to the naked eye.

Aphrodite   Greek goddess of love and beauty, identified with Venus of Roman mythology.

Apollo   The most glorious and beautiful of all the gods, Apollo was the divinity of the Sun and the god of medicine. He was the son of Jupiter and his mistress Latona (Leto), goddess of dark nights. Before Apollo's birth, Juno, jealous of her husband Jupiter, had banished Latona from Olympus to Earth, and forbad anyone, mortal or immortal, to give her comfort. Latona wandered the Earth and finally came to the sea, where she implored Neptune for help. He defied Juno by sending a dolphin to carry her to the island of Delos. It was here that Jupiter came to his mistress and conceived with her their twin children, Apollo and Diana.

Arachne   She was a mortal girl who fancied herself a better needlewoman even than Minerva, goddess of needlework. The girl's boasting eventually reached the goddess's ears, and she came down from Olympus, disguised as a crone, intending to persuade Arachne to desist. But the girl, unknowing, reiterated her claim that she could match even Minerva in a weaving contest, and this so angered the goddess she cast off her disguise and took up the challenge. Before long, Arachne could see she was utterly defeated, and in despair and shame crept away to hang herself with a rope. But Minerva was not willing to let the girl escape her eternal wrath. She turned the dying girl into a living spider, doomed to spin webs as flytraps for all time – a terrible warning to all conceited mortals.

Ares Greek god of war, identified with Mars of Roman mythology.

Argus A servant of Juno.

Athene When a great city began to be built by men in the Greek province of Attica, the gods looked on and began to vie with each other for the privilege of naming it. The last two in the bidding were Minerva, also known as Pallas Athena, and Neptune. To arbitrate between the two, Jupiter declared the privilege would go to the one who could create an object of the greatest use to mankind. Neptune at once crashed his trident into the ground, and up sprang a creature never before seen, a horse. All the gods were astounded at this powerful and versatile beast and doubted Minerva would be able to compete. But in her turn she summoned from the earth an olive tree. The gods scoffed, but she explained that as well as giving its wood, its fruit and its other material advantages, the olive also symbolised peace and prosperity – while the horse symbolised war. Jupiter gave her the prize, and the city became Athens.

Atlantis Lost civilisation of Greek mythology, sometimes taken to be the Minoan kingdom of Crete, swept away by a tidal wave in 1500BC.

Atlas Legendary king of Mauritania, he defied Perseus and was consequently transformed into Mount Atlas, bearing all the weight of the heavens on his head and hands.

Aurora Goddess of the dawn, she greeted Apollo, in the form of the Sun, every morning, by reaching her rosy fingers across the world in welcome. Also known as Eos, she married Tithonus, mortal prince of Troy, and persuaded the gods to grant him immortality. But she omitted to request eternal youth for her lover, and he grew old. He would have been an eternal burden on her had she not turned him into a grasshopper.

Bacchus Roman god of wine and revelry, identified with Greek Dionysus.

Caduceus Magic wand given by Apollo to Mercury, it had the power to reconcile enemies.

Callisto She was a maiden with whom Jupiter fell in love. The goddess Juno, Jupiter's jealous wife, took revenge by turning the girl into a bear, driving her from her home and into the dark forests. After years of searching, Jupiter found the former Callisto, and learned she had borne him a son, born as a bear and called Arcas. Jupiter took pity on them and lifted them from the forest into the heavens, where they are still known as the constellations of the Great Bear and Little Bear.

Cassandra Daughter of Priam, ruler of Troy, she was given the power by Apollo to foretell future events in exchange for a promise of surrendering her virtue. But she reneged, and the god blighted the gift by ordaining that no one should believe her prophecies.

Cerberus Three-headed guard dog at the gate to Hades.

Ceres Roman goddess of the earth's fruit, in particular corn (cereals). She was sister to Jupiter and bore him a daughter, Proserpina. Corresponds to Demeter in Greek legend.

Chaos Before the creation of the Earth and mankind, the shapeless mass of the universe was ruled by a blind and careless god called Chaos. With his wife Nox (Night), he ruled in utter darkness until he was overthrown by his son Erebus (Darkness), who then married his mother. They had two children, Ether (Light) and Hemera (Day), whose radiance threw the first light on the universe. Seeing the condition of Chaos's legacy, Ether and Hemera, now married to each other, dethroned their parents and set about creating the world from the disorder. It was their child Eros (Love) who made the Earth beautiful, firing his arrows into the world's cold heart to cause the plants and trees to grow, animals and birds to populate the land and fish to teem in the sea.

Charon   Ferryman who delivered the souls of the dead across the Styx to the Underworld.

Clio   See Muses.

Cronus   Also known as Saturn, he was the one among the 12 Titans who dared challenge his father, Uranus, the supreme being. Overthrowing Uranus, he heeded his father's warning that he too would in turn be overthrown by a son by eating every baby born to his wife (and sister Titan) Rhea. But Rhea finally deceived Cronus by having a child in secret. This was to be Jupiter, who grew up and overthrew Cronus. He also forced the former patriarch to regurgitate all the siblings he had swallowed, and thus were born Neptune, Pluto, Vesta, Ceres and Juno.

Cupid   Roman god of love, identified with Greek Eros.

Cyclops   Mythical giant shepherds of Sicily, in some stories described as having one eye only, in the centre of the forehead. See Polyphemus.

Daedalus   Athenian craftsman of legend, he avoided a death sentence for murder by fleeing to Crete, where he built the Labyrinth in which the monstrous Minotaur, offspring of King Minos's queen Pasiphaë's union with a bull, was confined. Later, Daedalus offended the king, and to escape from the island he fashioned wings for himself and his son Icarus. But while Daedalus himself had a successful flight, Icarus drowned, because he flew too close to the sun, melting the wax that held the wings in place, and fell into the sea.

Daphne   A nymph pursued by Apollo, she was terrified and fled, calling on her father, the river god Peneus, to save her – which he did, by transforming her into a laurel tree just as Apollo caught up with her. A chastened Apollo decreed that the laurel should henceforth be associated with his name, and that its glossy leaves be used for wreaths made to honour poets, musicians and other high achievers.

Delphi   Greek site of the temple and oracle of Apollo.

Diana   Roman goddess of hunting and the Moon. In Greek mythology as Artemis, she was the twin sister of Apollo and also known variously as Cynthia, Phoebe and Selene.

Dido   Mythical founder of Carthage and lover, according to Virgil, of Aeneas.

Dionysus   Greek god of fertility and wine, the son of Jupiter and mortal Semele.

Echo   In Greek legend a mountain nymph who distracted jealous Hera to help Jupiter conduct an illicit love affair. Hera punished her by depriving her of any power of speech other than to repeat the last words uttered by others. She subsequently fell in love with Narcissus but when rebuffed faded away until nothing remained but her voice.

Endymion   Young shepherd loved by Diana.

Epimetheus   See *Pandora*.

Eros   Greek god of love, variously said to be the son of Chaos, and of Jupiter and Aphrodite. In later mythology, he is identified with Cupid.

Ether   See *Chaos*.

Europa   A maiden seduced by Jupiter, he lured her by turning himself into a bull and persuading her to ride on his back. Her carried her across the sea to a new land he decided to name in her honour.

Fama   An attendant of Jupiter, she was the hundred-tongued goddess of fame, her task to proclaim Jupiter's wishes to the world.

Fortuna   An attendant of Jupiter, she was the goddess of luck, always poised on a revolving wheel, carelessly dispensing gifts to mankind.

Gaea   Goddess of the earth, she was the daughter of Ether and Hemera, and created Uranus, god of heaven. She married him and bore him 12 children, the Titans.

Gorgon   Monster of the underworld. There were three, most notably Medusa, with snakes for hair, and a gaze that turned to stone whoever looked at them.

Hades   Greek god of the underworld (also called Pluto), and the name given to his kingdom.

Harmonia   In Greek myth, the daughter of Ares and Aphrodite.

Harpies   In Greek myth, wind-spirits who abducted mortals, perhaps transporting them to the underworld. In later myths such as the Argonauts, they are portrayed as bird-like monsters with women's faces.

Hebe   Daughter of Zeus and Hera or, as that of Jupiter and Juno, Juventas.

Hector   Prince of Troy and the principal hero of the defence of the city. He killed Patroclus, and was in turn cut down by the avenging Achilles.

Helen   In Greek myth, the daughter of Leda, conceived with Zeus in the guise of a swan, and the most beautiful of all women. She became the wife of Menelaus, king of Sparta, but was seduced by Paris and carried off to Troy, precipitating the war. On Paris's death she briefly married his brother but after the fall of Troy was reconciled to Menelaus and returned with him to Sparta.

Helios   Greek god of the sun.

Hemera   See *Chaos*.

Hera   In Greek myth the daughter of Cronus and Rhea and both sister and wife to Zeus. The chief pre-hellenic deity of Argos, as goddess of female life and marriage.

Hercules   Roman name for Greek hero-god Heracles. A son of Zeus by Alcmene of Thebes, he had many adventures, beginning with the killing of a lion that was ravaging the cattle herds of a neighbouring king, Thespius. The hero wore the skin of the lion for ever after. He sailed on Troy, submitted himself to the Twelve Labours and after his death was elevated to Olympus, where he joined the immortals in marriage to Hebe, daughter of Hera.

Hermes   In Greek myth, the son of Zeus and Maia, identified with Mercury of Roman myth, and messenger of the gods. In earliest worship at Arcadia he was a god of fertility, and subsequently of travellers, of commerce and of athleticism.

Hermione   In Greek myth, the daughter of Menelaus and Helen.

Hyacinthus   He was a young mortal befriended by Apollo. But he was also admired by Zephyrus, god of the south wind. Jealous at seeing Hyacinthus and Apollo playing quoits together, Zephyrus blew Apollo's quoit violently off course, killing the youth. Apollo could not save him, but ordained a species of plant that grew from the blood-stained soil where Hyacinthus had fallen.

Icarus   Son of Daedalus.

Io   Daughter of river god Inachus courted by Jupiter but turned into a heifer by jealous Juno, who sent a giant gadfly to torment her – driving her into the sea thenceforth known as the Ionian. As the heifer, she swam to Egypt and was restored by Jupiter. They had a son, Epaphus, founder of Memphis.

Janus   Roman god of gates or openings. The year opens with the month of January.

Jason   Prince of Greek legend promised his rightful kingdom by the usurper Pelias if he could bring him a golden fleece. Jason, sailing in the ship Argo, succeeded, and married the sorceress Medea. But the couple were robbed of the kingdom by Pelias's heirs and fled to Corinth, where Jason abandoned Medea. She murdered their children and fled, and Jason committed suicide.

Jocasta   Mother of Oedipus.

Juno   Wife of Jupiter.

Jupiter   Roman god of gods, he was the son of Uranus and Rhea. Identified with Zeus of Greek myth.

Juventas   Also known as Hebe, an attendant of Jupiter and the goddess of youth. She was Jupiter's cup bearer, always ready to pour out the nectar of the gods.

Laertes   Legendary king of Ithaca and father of Odysseus.

Laocoön   Trojan priest of Apollo who warned his countrymen against accepting the Greeks' gift of a wooden horse. Apollo feared the Trojans would heed the priests' warnings, and sent sea monsters to kill Laocoön, and his sons.

Laius   Father of Oedipus.

Mars Son of Jupiter and Juno, god of war, identified with Ares of Greek myth.

Medea Wife of Jason.

Medusa The only mortal among the Gorgons, killed by Perseus. From her blood sprang Pegasus, the winged horse.

Menelaus Legendary king of Sparta, brother of Agamemnon and husband of Helen.

Mercury Son and special messenger of Jupiter, he was born in Arcadia of Maia. Also known as Hermes and Psychopompus and as the god of commerce, eloquence, rain, wind and thieves.

Midas Legendary king of Phrygia, he was promised one wish by the god Dionysus and asked that everything he might touch would turn to gold. But the gift was a curse, because even Midas's food metallised at his touch and he faced starvation. Dionysus revoked the wish and Midas was saved.

Minerva Roman counterpart of Pallas Athene, born of Jupiter in unusual circumstances. Jupiter had a headache so bad he had his son Vulcan cleave his head open with an axe. From the fissure emerged a full-grown Minerva, wearing armour and carrying a spear. She was the goddess of peace, defensive war – and needlework – as well as being the incarnation of wisdom. Her first task was to drive out Dulness, the goddess who had hitherto presided over the world.

Minotaur Monstrous offspring of Pasiphaë, wife of King Minos of Knossos (Crete) and a bull. Confined by Minos in the Labyrinth, the Minotaur was killed by Theseus.

Muses Nine daughters of Jupiter and Mnemosyne and patronesses of the arts: Calliope (heroic poetry), Clio (history), Erato (lyric poetry), Euterpes (song), Melpomene (tragedy), Terpsichore (dance), Thalia (pastoral poetry).

Oedipus Legendary king of Thebes. Only son of King Laius and Jocasta, he was abandoned as a newborn on a mountainside after Laius was told by an oracle he would be killed by his own son. But Oedipus did not die. He was rescued by a shepherd and taken to Corinth. When he grew up, he learned from the oracle that his fate would be to kill his father and marry his mother. Through a series of twists of fate, these terrible predictions came true.

Myrmidons   Legendary race of Greece who served Peleus and his son Achilles.

Naiads   Greek nymphs of fresh water.

Narcissus   In Greek legend, the son of a river god who rejected the love of Echo, preferring the reflection of his own image in the water. In vengeance for his cruelty to Echo, the god Nemesis caused him to fall in love with his reflection, which he took to be a beautiful water nymph but could not capture. He pined away at the pool side and was changed into the flower that bears his name.

Nemesis   Greek goddess who apportioned joy and grief to mortals and brought downfall on those who prospered too well.

Neptune   Roman god of water, later associated with Poseidon, Greek god of the sea.

Nike   Greek goddess of victory, daughter of Pallas Athene and Styx.

Nyx   In Greek myth, the daughter of Chaos and personification of night. Corresponds to Roman Nox.

Oceanus   Greek god of the river believed to circle the world. Sometimes called the father of all the gods, but also described as the son of Uranus.

Odysseus   In Greek legend, the son of Laertes and Anticleia. With Penelope, he was the father of Telemachus. Odysseus joined the Greek expedition against Troy and distinguished himself in strategy and battle. His long journey home to Ithaca after the fall of Troy is described in Homer's *Odyssey*.

Olympia   The people of Greece built a great temple to Zeus at Olympia. Every five years, they celebrated the god's victory over the Titans by holding games there.

Olympus   To the Greeks, the Earth was a disc rather than a sphere, and at the very centre of that disc lay Greece. And on the summit of Olympus, the highest mountain of Greece – the highest point of the world – resided Zeus and his fellow gods.

Orion   A hunter who came upon the Pleiades and passionately pursued them. They fled in fear, appealing to Diana to help them escape, which she did by turning them into white pigeons. Orion, who was always accompanied by his faithful hunting dog Sirius, subsequently became the lover of Diana, but she was deceived into killing him with one of her arrows by her disapproving brother Apollo. So that she would never forget the luckless Orion, she had him conveyed to the heavens as a constellation – along with the loyal Sirius.

Orpheus   Poet and musician of Greek myth, sometimes referred to as the son of Calliope (see Muses) and Apollo. He wooed and won Eurydice and they shared an idyllic life in the forest – until she was fatally bitten by a poisonous snake. Orpheus could not save her and her spirit descended into Hades. The heart-broken Orpheus persuaded Jupiter to allow him to go into the Underworld in a bid to retrieve Eurydice. With his divine playing, he beguiled Cerberus, the three-headed guard dog at the gate, and eventually made his way into the presence of Pluto and Prosperina, rulers of Hades. They reluctantly agreed Euridyce could leave, but only on condition that Orpheus trusted their word to the extent he would not look back until he had departed their kingdom. Orpheus willingly agreed, but just a few steps short of the upper world, forgot his word and turned his gaze back – only to see the figure of his beloved Eurydice fading back into the depths.

Pandora   In the Greek myth of creation, the gods populated the Earth with mortal men, and after a while decided to add woman. Just as Eve followed Adam, Pandora was fashioned by the gods as companion to the first mortal, Epimetheus. They lived in a state of innocent bliss until one day the god Mercury dropped in, carrying a heavy box, which he left in the couple's care. Pandora possessed a feminine curiosity, and while Epimetheus was out of sight, and thinking she heard pleading voices from inside the box, she opened it. Out flew all the ills that from that moment blighted the life of man – the likes of sickness and envy, greed and anger – in the form of horrid, moth-like creatures, before Pandora could slam down the lid. But there was redemption. One remaining voice within the box pleaded for release, and fortunately Pandora had the courage to release it. This last, redeeming, creature was Hope.

Paris   In Greek legend the second son of King Priam of Troy and younger brother of Hector. His mother, Hecuba, had a vision before his birth that he would bring destruction on Troy and as a baby he was left out on Mount Ida to die of exposure. But a shepherd found him, gave him the name Paris and taught him to be a courageous defender of flocks and their shepherds. He then discovered his true birth and was taken back by Priam. He married Oenone, daughter of a river god, but soon abandoned her for Helen, wife of Menelaus, king of Sparta, whom he carried away to Troy – precipitating the ten-year Trojan war, in which Paris was defeated by Menelaus in a fight outside the walls of the city, but survived through the protection of Aphrodite. Paris killed Achilles with an arrow shot to his vulnerable heel and in turn himself died from an arrow wound after he returned wounded to Oenone, who refused to nurse him. Paris had won the protection of Aphrodite in the 'judgement' – a beauty contest between her and rival goddesses Hera and Athena in which he awarded the prize, a golden apple inscribed with 'to the fairest,' to Aphrodite.

Penelope   Wife of Odysseus. During her husband's long absence from their Ithaca home at Troy and afterwards, she was wooed by increasingly numerous and insistent suitors but kept them at bay by saying she could not contemplate marriage before she completed a robe she was weaving for Odysseus's father, Laertes. She weaved all day, but unpicked all the work at night. Her husband returned just in time to rescue her from the suitors, all of whom he killed with arrows.

Persephone   In Greek myth, the daughter of Demeter, goddess of the earth's fruits, conceived with her brother Zeus. When Persephone grew up, Zeus promised her to the god of the underworld, Pluto, who claimed her. But Zeus did not tell Demeter, and the goddess was so angry she quit Olympus to live on earth among the mortals. In her anger, she blighted the harvests. To placate her Zeus sent Hermes into the underworld to retrieve Persephone. A compromise was reached in which Persephone spent the fallow part of the year with Pluto and the remainder on Olympus with her mother and father.

Perseus   In Greek myth the son of Danaë, princess of Argos, and Zeus. A suitor of Danaë contrived to get rid of her protective son by sending him on a seemingly impossible mission to obtain the head of the Medusa, which he succeeded in doing, amidst many other adventures. He married Andromeda.

Pleiades   The daughters of Atlas, they were the seven nymphs of Diana. Pursued by the hunter Orion, they fled in fear and appealed to Diana to help them escape. The goddess obliged by turning them into white pigeons, and later conducted them into the heavens, where they formed a brilliant constellation. But when Troy fell, their stars dimmed and one was extinguished altogether.

Pluto   God of the underworld, also known as the god Hades.

Polyphemus   Cyclops and son of Poseidon who captured Odysseus and his followers, killing and eating several of them before Odysseus blinded his single eye and escaped.

Pomona   Roman goddess of gardens and orchards.

Poseidon   Greek god of the sea, identified with Roman Neptune.

Priam   King of Troy at the time of the Trojan war. His wife Hecuba bore him nineteen children, including Hector and Paris.

Prometheus   The source of today's 'Promethean' – as in a skilful or daringly innovative person or idea – Prometheus was a well-intentioned demigod in the Greek mythological version of the creation of mankind. To help man in his struggle to survive, Prometheus stole fire from Mount Olympus and passed it on to the mortals. But Jupiter was enraged by the theft and punished Prometheus by having him chained on a rock in the Caucasus mountains. Every day, a vulture came and tore at Prometheus's liver, devouring it. At night, as the vulture slept, the liver grew back. Prometheus suffered this punishment for many centuries until Hercules, a son of Jupiter, came to the mountain, killed the vulture and broke the prisoner's chains.

Proserpina   In Roman myth, wife of Pluto and goddess of the Underworld. Counterpart of Persephone.

Proteus   A minor Greek sea-god who could change his appearance at will. Protean today denotes a person who can change or adapt to differing conditions.

Psyche   In Greek myth, a princess personifying the human soul. In the legend, her beauty was envied by Aphrodite, who instructed the god Cupid to dupe Psyche into loving a most cruel and hideous man. But instead, Cupid fell in love with Psyche himself. After many setbacks, the couple were finally reconciled with Aphrodite. Psyche was elevated to the immortals and lived in unending bliss with Cupid.

Pygmalion   Legendary king of Cyprus who made sculptures only of the gods until he fashioned the image of a mortal woman and then fell in love with her. He persuaded Venus to give life to the stone figure, and the couple lived happily ever after.

Rhea   One of the Titans, wife of Cronus and mother of Zeus.

Romulus and Remus   Boys born of an illicit union between Mars and Vestal Virgin Ilia. She paid the price of breaking her vows – burial alive – and the children were cast out into the forest to be devoured by wild beasts. But they were adopted by a she-wolf, and went on to found Rome.

Saturn   Roman name for Cronus, he was leader of the 12 Titans born to Uranus and Gaea and overthrew his father, only to be displaced in his own turn by his son Jupiter.

Satyrs   In Greek myth, woodland creatures portrayed as half man, half beast and identified with the sensual cult of Dionysus.

Semel   Mortal princess seduced by Zeus who gave birth to Dionysus and died in the process.

Sirens   Sea nymphs of Greek myth who lured sailors to destruction with their irresistible song.

Sisyphus   Legendary founder of Corinth whose greed was punished in Hades. His eternal task was to push a marble boulder up a steep hill, only for it to roll back just short of the top.

Talaria   Winged sandals given by the gods to Mercury, their messenger, to speed his motion.

Tantalus   In Greek myth a legendary king and son of Zeus who was punished by the gods for revealing their secrets or, in another version of the legend, for murdering his own son. His punishment was to stand up to his neck in fresh water, but whenever he inclined his head to drink, it retreated from him. And above his head was suspended a bunch of succulent fruit, which the wind blew out of his reach whenever he tried to grasp it.

Tartarus   The underworld, presided over by Pluto.

Terminus   Roman god of frontiers and boundaries.

Theseus   Legendary king of Athens, he went voluntarily as one of the seven youths and seven maidens sent by the city in tribute to Crete to be devoured by the Minotaur. Ariadne, daughter of Crete's King Minos, helped Theseus kill the Minotaur, and the couple sailed away to Naxos, where Theseus abandoned her and went on to many more adventures.

Titans   The 12 children of Uranus and Gaea. The Titans' immense strength intimidated their father, who feared they might overthrow him. So he had them chained in a dark abyss called Tartarus. But their mother Gaea pitied them and went down into the abyss to persuade them to escape and seize power from Uranus. Only one of the 12, Cronus – also known as Saturn and Time – was willing to challenge his father. In the great conflict that ensued, Cronus defeated Uranus, but not before the father had warned the son that he, in turn, would be overthrown by his own son. Cronus, as supreme being, released his siblings, the other 11 Titans, and ruled with them. From among them he married his sister Rhea.

Ulysses   Roman counterpart of Odysseus.

Uranus   The god of heaven and supreme being, created by Gaea, goddess of the land. She married Uranus and bore him 12 children, the Titans (see Titans).

Venus   Roman goddess identified with Greek Aphrodite.

Vulcan   Roman god of fire, and son of Jupiter and Juno.

Zephyrus God of the west wind.

Zeus Supreme god of Greek mythology, he was a son of Cronus and Rhea, and dwelt on Mount Olympus with his wife Hera, one of his sisters. When Zeus and his brother Titans overthrew Cronus and divided the ruling of the world between them, Hades took the underworld, Poseidon the sea and Zeus the heights and heavens, with the earth shared between them. But Zeus, from Olympus, came to rule over all, becoming the supreme law-giver, and with control even over Fate. He fathered many children besides the two born to Hera. Identified with Roman Jupiter.

Clerihew A comic poem, usually of just two rhyming but not scanning couplets and devoted to someone well-known. Originated by Edmund Clerihew Bentley (1875–1956).

> Edmund Clerihew Bentley
> Mocked poetry gently
> By devising a verse form
> Erring by a syllable or two from the norm.

cliché In the original 19th-century French, a *cliché* was a printer's plate or block, giving rise to the figurative use of the word to describe something that is much repeated. A cliché is a phrase born respectable, but grown hackneyed by overuse or misapplication. Terms such as 'cutting edge' or 'state of the art' are examples. Both began as usefully resonant references to inspired innovation but very soon became mere embellishments of the old word 'new.' Clichés proliferate in the language of politics, commerce, sport and show business. Speakers persist with 'at this moment in time' (in other words, now) in hope of adding gravitas to their words, or reach for the likes of 'you don't have to be a rocket scientist to understand this' in an endeavour to persuade audiences that they have both a sense of humour and a grip on the current argot. In the written word, clichés are inexcusable, but even the best-known authors may not be immune. Bill Bryson, who writes about the use of language as well as on travel, was rightly taken to task by a critic over his bestseller on Australia, *Down Under*, published in 2000: "the

climatic

book is larded with clichés ('holding centre stage'; 'on the face of the earth'; 'stopped me in my tracks')." Writers should be aware of movie mogul Sam Goldwyn's immortal maxim: "I avoid clichés like the plague."

These are some of the worst offenders in current use:

At the end of the day	Movers and shakers
The big picture	Move the goal posts
The bottom line	No win situation
Can do	The only game in town
Go the extra mile	Paradigm shift
The jury is still out	Pared to the bone
In line with best practice	Sea change
In this day and age	Stretching the envelope
Leave no stone unturned	To be honest
Level playing field	Touch base
Let me make this perfectly clear	Win win situation

click(s) and mortar   Recent term for a retail business combining online activity with physical premises.

climatic   It means of climate, as in "global warning is causing climatic changes." Do not confuse with climactic, meaning of climax, as in "the story's climactic moment."

climax   See crescendo.

closure   A word that has lately acquired several new applications. Originally meaning simply the act of closing, or the end of a session (in particular the closing vote in a Parliamentary debate) it has more recently come to encompass the various stoppers used for drinks bottles – corks (natural or synthetic), screwcaps and crown caps can all safely be called closures – and in marketing speak, the act of completing a sale. Most recently, closure has entered the jargon once known as 'psychobabble.' It describes the resolution of emotional experiences, in particular grief. Thus, the phrase used by New York City officials on welcoming visitors to the viewing platform erected in 2002 at the site of the former World Trade Centre, destroyed in a terrorist attack in the previous year: "The city of New York has built this so you can view and come to closure."

coca   A South American shrub (*Erythroxylon coca*) from which the narcotic-stimulant drug cocaine is obtained. No relation to cocoa, the seed pod of the cacao tree from which chocolate is obtained.

Coca-Cola   Trademark. 'Cola drink' is OK to describe brown, sweetened beverages of the genre that are of uncertain brand.

Cockney rhyming slang   In medieval England, the word cockney developed from 'cock's egg' – a term for an undersized hen's egg, and thus for a dwarfish, malformed or idiot child. By the 1500s, it was a common term among country dwellers for that growing section of the population who had taken the inconceivable step of living in a town. And by the 1600s, Cockney – with an initial capital – had become specific to people who lived in London, in particular those born within earshot of the church bells of St Mary-le-Bow in the east of the city. The famous rhyming slang was allegedly first used by Cockney traders in London markets to conceal the true content of verbal exchanges concerning confidential or even criminal matters, but it seems more likely this arcane language was developed for no more than innocent amusement. Although the Cockney terms are almost invariably phrases of two or more words, it is very common for only the first word to be used, as in "I'm on the dog (phone)" or "My plates (feet) are killing me." This is what can make much Cockney slang so very hard to grasp. These are a few of the enduring rhymes:

Adam and Eve – believe	daisy root – boot
apples and pears – stairs	dicky dirt – shirt
Barnet fair – hair	dog and bone – telephone
boat race – face	frog and toad – road
Brahms and Liszt – pissed	half inch – pinch
bricks and mortar – daughter	Jack and Jill – pill
butcher's hook – look	jam jar – car
currant bun – sun	Lady Godiva – fiver

Cockney School

Mutt and Jeff – deaf	raspberry (tart) – fart
plates of meat – feet	tea leaf – thief
porkie (from pork pie) – lie	trouble and strife – wife
raspberry (ripple) – nipple	

Cockney School   Nickname given by the versifier and waspish critic John Lockhart to a circle of London writers in the early 1800s, including William Hazlitt, Leigh Hunt and the 'Cockney' poet John Keats.

cognate   In linguistics, cognates are words in different languages with common derivations. English 'uncle' is a cognate of French *oncle* because both words derive from Latin *aunculus*.

cognitive   Buzz word. Cognition is a fancy word for constructive thoughtfulness – reasoning, in effect. Most used in the context of 'cognitive therapy' in which the therapist challenges the patient's unconstructive thoughts.

coke   A fuel extracted from coal or, more likely in the 21st century, a term for cocaine. The word Coke with an initial capital is a trademark of the Coca-Cola Corporation.

collective nouns   Are words such as couple, group and mob to be treated as singular or plural? Writers differ on use, as in "a married couple was reported missing last night" or "a married couple were ... " Strictly speaking, collective nouns are singular. It is correct to say the couple is, not the couple are. But problems soon arise. You write "the couple was missing" but in the next sentence want to add that a search has started for the couple – and cannot sensibly write "the police are looking for it." You must write "them." If you believe this makes a nonsense of using the collective word in the singular, you may be right. It is one of the countless quirks of English usage that looks set to remain unresolved for a few centuries yet.

colloquial   Describing informal or familiar English, as distinct from formal or literary English. Latin *com* (with) and *loqui* (to speak).

colon   When writing down direct speech, use this punctuation mark where the speaker is identified at the beginning of the sentence, as in "He said: 'Hello.' " Use the colon also to introduce lists, as in "She brought with her some essential items: bread, cheese, a bottle of wine."

In the 21st century, the colon retains little of its former function as a kind of dramatic stop, as "The wound was severe: blood issued freely from it." This role has now been taken over by the semicolon (*qv*). But the colon still has its use as a pause in a sentence in which a second clause is entirely a fulfilment of the expectations created by the first. "He flung open the front door: she rushed into his arms."

Should the first word after a colon take an initial capital? Only where that word is the beginning of a new sentence, as in reported speech.

combat   Once a mere noun, combat is now in common use as a verb, and presents problems with conjugation. Dictionaries fudge the issue by claiming that both combating and combatting are correct (and combated and combatted as well). But they specify only combatant and combative. What to do? Stick to the single 't' because there is no earthly reason why combating and combative should take different forms.

comedy   A narrative of an amusing kind, usually with a happy ending. In the earliest days of English drama, comedy was any play that was not a tragedy, in keeping with the Greek tradition. Refinements on the theme now include black comedy, of an ironic kind, and comedy of manners, in which the conventions of social behaviour are ridiculed. Greek *komos* (revel).

comma   Of all the punctuation marks, the comma is the most frequently used – and misused. Its function is to insert a pause or separation between words or phrases where it will assist the reader in making sense of what is written. The power of the comma is graphically illustrated in the title of journalist-playwright Lynne Truss's bestselling book of 2003 on punctuation, *Eats, Shoots and Leaves*. Illustrated on the original cover with a picture of a panda munching bamboo, the title might have been expected to be *Eats Shoots and Leaves*. But the addition of the comma utterly alters the sense to suggest a book in which someone has a meal, discharges a firearm, and then departs.

When it comes to using the comma correctly and constructively, do pay heed to this demonstration of its influence. A comma is a pause, an opportunity to take a breath, and where no pause or breath is called for, don't use it.

Use commas when listing, and make use of the 'Oxford comma' at the end of the list – that, is before the 'and' preceding the last item. An example is "at the motor show we saw Ferraris, Lamborghinis, Maseratis, and a Ford Mondeo."

But don't use 'splice' commas to extend sentences. Several short sentences are better than one long sentence, every time. The following sentence, for example, is senselessly strung out: 'When she got home, she realised she had forgotten her key, then remembered she had left a spare one under the doormat, so she found it, and let herself in.' Much better to write, in exactly the same words: 'When she got home she realised she had forgotten her key. Then she remembered she had left a spare one under the doormat. She found it and let herself in.'

Common Prayer, Book of   A landmark not just in the form of Christian worship but in the history of the English language, it was the first service book published in English rather than Latin. It was consequently the first printed book of any kind that millions of English speakers ever saw in their own language. The first edition, begun during the tumultuous separation of Henry VIII's Church of England from Rome, was published in 1549. It conveys the full liturgical effect of the Reformation in England, with the Catholic Mass transforming into the Protestant Communion. Much of the original work, and subsequent revisions, were carried out by the Archbishop of Canterbury, Thomas Cranmer, who died a martyr's death at the stake for his Anglican beliefs under the papal terror imposed by Queen Mary I in 1556.

common sense   Two words, but when in use as an adjective, write it as one word, as 'he found a commonsense solution to the problem.'

comparative In grammar, adjectives and adverbs have comparative (and superlative) forms, as in big, bigger (and biggest).

compare There is a difference between 'compare to' and 'compare with.' In the phrase "my garden is small compared to yours," the two gardens are compared on size alone. Where a more qualitative, analytical comparison is being made, the phrase might be "my garden hardly compares with yours."

comparative literature You can study this at university, if you have nothing better to do. A 19th-century invention, it is the pursuit of comparing the literature of different nations or races.

compass points There are several options for writing points such as North East. The possible variations are northeast, north east, north-east, Northeast, North east and North-east. The principal rule is to be consistent, especially when describing formally defined regions, such as the North East of England. Where the description is less specific, the use of initial capitals might be inappropriate, as the south west of the United States.

complement In grammar, a word or phrase qualifying a verb and completing the predicate (*qv*) of a sentence. In the phrase 'man bites dog savagely,' the parts are: man (subject), bites dog (predicate), savagely (complement).

complement and **compliment** A complement is something that makes up a number. A compliment is an expression of admiration. Complementary means completing, in the sense of "the sauce complements the meat." Complimentary means either in praise or given as a courtesy, as in "a complimentary glass of wine with your meal."

compound nouns Formed of two or more other words, they can present a problem in the plural. Most simply take the 's' after the last word, as in forget-me-nots and line-outs. But where the noun denotes a person it is the person rather than the prepositional phrase or adverb that takes the 's' – as in comrades in arms and mothers-in-law, passers-by and runners-up.

comprise Transitive verb meaning to include or consist of a precise number. Not to be confused with compose. 'The team

conceit

comprised just six players' is correct. 'The team is comprised of 11 players' is incorrect.

conceit   In literature, a conceit is a device in a narrative that is intended to spring a witty surprise on readers or audiences, usually via an outlandish metaphor. Conceits are a feature particularly of 16th and 17th century literature, exemplified by poet Robert Herrick's famed injunction to a mistress to seize the opportunity for love while still young enough to enjoy it – meaning, of course, that she should do so while she will still please her lecherous, ageing suitor:

> Gather ye rosebuds while ye may,
> Old Time is still a-flying

Today, literary critics are inclined to describe any particularly felicitous phrase as a conceit, meaning that it is well-contrived and amusing, but perhaps trivial. Don't confuse this kind of conceit with the behaviour of an annoyingly vain or proud person. Latin *conceptus* (a concept).

confessional   Fiction, drama or poetry described as confessional is supposedly written by an author seeking to reveal secrets of his or her own life, perhaps in hope of some kind of absolution. As new authors increasingly transform into 'celebrities' in the 21st century, we may all have to resign ourselves to more of this sort of thing.

confidant(e)   In fiction and drama, this is the character to whom the hero or heroine confides intimate thoughts, thus revealing them to the audience. It's a French word, so add the 'e' for female confidantes.

conjugation   In Latin and subsequently in English, the system of showing the inflections of verbs, as in the present-tense conjugation of the Latin verb *amare*, to love: *amo* (I love), *amas* (you love), *amat* (he/she loves), *amamus* (we love), *amatis* (you in the plural love), *amant* (they love). Irregular verbs both in Latin and English are so known because they conjugate in an irregular way, as in *sum* (I am), *est* (he is) etc.

consonant   The letters of the alphabet are divided into two groups, the five vowels a, e, i, o and u, and the 21 consonants.

consonance   As a device usually in poetry, the use of a succession of identical consonants with different vowel sounds, as in the "plink, plank, plunk, plonk" of dripping water.

contraction   The shrinking of one or more words to one shorter word. 'Won't' is a contraction of 'will not' and 'motel' is a contraction of 'motor' and 'hotel.' See also portmanteau words.

cool   Street word for anything fashionable or admirable, thought to originate with the jazz movement in the United States early in the 20th century. It has entered the 21st century in vigorous currency, but should be avoided in formal written work.

co-operative   Use the hyphen. The various Co-operative societies founded in the 19th century still spell their names with a hyphen, and it makes sense to be consistent.

copy   In publishing, the author's original text.

copyright   An author's entitlement not to have his or her work published without permission and/or payment. It is widely believed that all authors own the copyright in everything they have done, but it is very common for publishers to purchase work outright for a one-off payment. Ownership of copyright stays with the author or other party for the whole of the author's life and, under European Union law, for 70 years afterwards.

cotch   Current Metropolitan slang word with meaning similar to chill, or relax.

couple   Describing two people together, this is a collective word and a singular one. But which is correct: "a couple has gone missing" or "a couple have gone missing"? In this case, use the first phrase, because the singular verb makes it clear the couple is indeed a couple. The second version is less clear. Does it refer back to a previous phrase describing what constituted this couple – a couple of *what* have gone missing?

couplet   Pair of lines in verse, rhyming or otherwise.

-cracy and **-crat**   Suffix denoting a particular kind of rule or influence, as in autocracy and autocrat – the wielding of power by an individual, or the individual in question. There are many variations: aristocrat (a member of the nobility), bureaucrat (an official, usually of an inflexible type), plutocrat (a person with influence through wealth), democracy (rule by representatives elected by the population) and theocracy (rule by unelected clergy). New ones are continually being coined: eurocrat (European bureaucrat), meritocrat (influential person owing position to ability rather than social class), adhocracy (rule hastily established by an invader, usually American) and gerontocracy (government by the elderly, often applied to the Communist Party regime in China). You can even make up your own: gastrocrat (dictator of culinary fashion). Greek *kratos* (power).

craic   Chatter, in Irish, as in "we went to Dublin just for the craic in the pubs."

crawss   A nonsense word, but a delightful one. It is the pronunciation of the word 'cross' (in the sense of mildly angry) allegedly used by the Queen, and exchanged in affectionate imitation within her own circle.

creature   A word subject to subtle nuances, its original sense is that of any living thing created (divinely or otherwise), from Latin *creare*, to create. But now it is commonly used to describe a person with the status of a lackey, as "the Prime Minister's creatures in the Cabinet." Curiously, the word can convey both esteem – 'a beautiful creature' – and contempt, as in 'a miserable creature.'

crescendo   In musical notation it describes a progressive increase in loudness. It has subsequently come to mean a rise in other respects, such as tension or violence. Beware confusion with 'climax,' as in the solecism (*qv*) "the din was rising to a crescendo." Italian from Latin *crescere* (to grow).

crevasse and **crevice**   A crevasse is a split in a glacier wide and deep enough to fall into. A crevice is a narrow opening in natural rock or stonework, just big enough to allow a handhold.

cringe   In the participle form, use cringeing (not cringing).

criteria   Plural form of the word criterion.

critic   A tricky word, it means both a person who makes objective evaluations, as in a literary critic, and one who expresses one-sided disapproval. This applies also to the use of criticize and criticism.

It is a shortcoming of the language, not yet remedied, that these words should have such diverse meanings. Use with care.

critical mass This cliché arises from the language of nuclear physics. It refers to the quantity of fissile material needed for a nuclear chain reaction, and has been adopted to mean, vaguely, any accumulation of momentum necessary to stimulating action. Avoid.

crypto- It has been trendy for some years to append this prefix to all sorts of words to form a pejorative sense, as 'cryptofascist.' When Prime Minister in the 1980s, Margaret Thatcher famously described then Labour Leader of the Opposition Neil Kinnock as a "cryptocommunist" and rekindled a craze that has lasted into the 21st century. The prefix simply means secret or hidden, from Greek *kruptos* (concealed).

cul-de-sac A street with a closed end, from French 'bottom of bag' is not a term used in France. Editing a Millennium book about a Dorset village I came across the phrase "the three cul-de-sac of Woodland Mead, Dinhay and Ham Meadow." How to apply a correct plural? I plumped for culs-de-sac – the form this phrase would take in the plural in French (if it existed).

culinary words As topics of very widespread interest, food and cookery are bringing all sorts of exotic new words into regular use. Here are a few of the trickier ones, in terms either of spelling, sense, or both.

al dente – of pasta cooked firm to the bite (Italian)
antipasti – Italian hors d'oeuvres
aspic – clear jelly from fish or meat cooking juices
au gratin – food cooked with sauce, sprinkled with crumbs of
  bread and/or cheese and grilled (French)
avocado – large-stoned 'pear'
bain marie – pan of hot water in which smaller pan is heated
  (French)
biltong – South African dried meat
blanquette – meat stew in a creamy sauce (French)
borscht – Russian beetroot soup

culinary words

bouillabaisse – French fish stew

brûlé – dessert topped with glazed sugar (French)

cantucini – Italian sweet biscuit

carbonnade – beef stew with beer (French)

cassoulet -French bean stew

chorizo – Spanish sausage

ciabatta – a kind of Italian bread

civet – game stew (French)

coquille – scallop (French)

daube – stew of meat and vegetables (French)

durum – a kind of wheat

enchilada – Mexican filled tortilla

entrée – once, the third course in a banquet. Now, a main
   course (French)

escalope – thin slice of meat, flattened and fried (French)

faggot – small patty of seasoned pork offal

felafel – Arab fried patty of chick peas

foie gras – preserved whole 'fat liver' of duck or goose (French)

fricassee – sauced-based dish of fowl or game

galantine – jellied meat

garam masala – Indian spice mixture

gazpacho – chilled Spanish vegetable soup

gelato – Italian ice cream

gnocchi – Italian potato pasta

goujon – gudgeon, a tiny fish, or other meat or fish cut to the
   same shape (French)

goulash – Hungarian beef stew with onion, tomato and paprika

grecque, à la – in the Greek style, with stock and olive oil or
   garnished with rice

grissini – Italian breadsticks

guacamole – Latin avocado dish

hominy – American maize porridge

hummus – Arab chick-pea purée

jugged – stewed in a covered pot (especially hare)

jus – juices from cooking meat used as sauce (French)

kedgeree – Anglo-Indian dish of rice, fish, eggs and flavourings

meunière – miller's wife, as in fish fried in butter and sprinkled with parsley and lemon juice (French)

navarin – French lamb stew

panetone – Italian cake-like Christmas bread

panforte – Italian sweet fruit cake

parfait – frozen dessert of whipped cream and fruit purée (French)

pease pudding – purée of cooked dried peas

penne – Italian pasta, resembling tubular quills

pilaf(f) – Persian spiced rice dish

pilau -Near East (especially Indian) spiced rice

pirozhki – Russian filled savoury pastries

pizzaiola -Italian meat dish in red wine, tomato and garlic

polenta – Italian maize porridge-slab

popadum – Asian crisp bread

prosciutto – Italian cured uncooked ham

provençale – cooked in the Provence manner, with garlic and tomatoes (French)

quenelle – French poached dumpling

rigatoni – Italian pasta, a ribbed form of macaroni

roux – fat and flour mixture as a sauce base (French)

salsa – Spanish sauce

shashlick – Russian kebab

succotash – American bean and cereal stew

sukiyaki – Japanese thin-sliced meat

sushi – Japanese cakes of rice and fish, vegetables etc

tabbouleh – Arab salad of cracked wheat and vegetables

tempura – Japanese deep-fried fish or vegetables

teriyaki – marinade for fish or meat (Japanese)

timbale – cooking mould and the item cooked in it (French)

vermicelli – Italian pasta in fine strands

yoghurt – treated, curdled milk

zabaglione – Italian egg, marsala and sugar dessert

currant and current

currant and **current**   A currant is a dried grape. A current is a flow of electrical charges. The adjective current means of the present time.

cygnet   swan chick. Beware misspelling as 'signet' as in the item of jewellery, once used to impress a signatory seal, known as a signet ring.

cymbal   Percussive musical instrument. Beware misspelling as 'symbol.'

cynic   It comes as a surprise to dictionary users that the widely misunderstood word cynic means 'dog-like' from its ancient Greek origin *kynos*, a dog. The Greeks adopted the word for people with the snarling, surly nature of a cur, and it is possible that the Cynics, the Athenian sect of philosophers founded by Antisthenes (*c.*455–*c.*360BC), derived its name from this source. The Cynics were notable for their manifest disdain for scholarship, art and entertainments and were characterised by their gloomy behaviour. The school where Antisthenes taught was called the *Kynosarges*, the hall of the dogs (or in some translations, the bastards). Today, the term cynic embraces anyone with a misanthropic, heartless or pessimistic nature.

   The distinction between a cynic and a sceptic has given much exercise to philologists. It is obvious enough, but it is worth recording one outstanding illustration, given by the Australian writer and sometime television critic Clive James (b 1939). A sceptic, he has written, is someone who believes TV soap operas are absurd; a cynic is someone who thinks other people don't.

czar and **tsar**   In Russian, the word is *tsar*, but its origin, amazingly enough, is Latin *Caesar*, from the first emperor of that name, Julius. The spelling czar is commemorative of the origin. Dictionaries do not express preferences between the two spellings, and even offer a third, tzar.

Dada   The early 20th-century Dada movement in art, literature and film ridiculed cultural and social conventions, and continues to be cited by writers even now as a defining form of anti-establishment nihilism. From the name of a review staged in the aftermath of the First World War, *dada* is a French word meaning a hobby-horse.

Damascene   Relating to the city of Damascus, capital of Syria, but best known in the phrase 'damascene conversion.' It derives from the story of St Paul, as related in his letter to the Corinthians in the New Testament. A Pharisee and persecutor of Christians, St Paul – then Saul of Tarsus – was on a journey from Jerusalem to Damascus for the trial of St Stephen when he saw a vision of God on the road and was converted to the Christian faith. So, a damascene conversion is now used to mean any sudden, diametric switch in allegiance, belief or taste. It might be heretical, but surely any biblical allusion is still welcome in our growingly secular world. Damascene also denotes a style of steel manufacture historically associated with Damascus, particularly the inlaying of gold or silver into metal products, such as weapons. A 'damascene sword' is thus a familiar term for a certain kind of Arabian inlaid ceremonial blade. Beware confusion with the Sword of Damocles (*qv*).

Damocles, Sword of   It refers to a situation of great risk, and derives from a tale told by Roman statesman Cicero. Damocles, he related, was an aristocrat in the court of ancient Greek tyrant of Syracuse, Dionysius the Elder, in the fourth century BC. Damocles was a great flatterer of the tyrant, but Dionysus regarded him with suspicion. Enjoying a feast at court one day, Damocles was reminded of the precariousness of his position at court when his host informed him that a sword, suspended by a single human hair, hung from the roof immediately above his head.

dark

dark Besides its familiar senses, it is used in the current Metropolitan slang as a synonym for good, as in "that was a really dark film."

Dark Ages In Britain, this era is widely taken to be the period between the end of the Roman occupation in the 5th century AD and the 9th century, when King Alfred established the first Christian sovereignty over much of England. Anglo-Saxon and Viking incursions during the period are taken to have plunged the country into the darkness of pagan disorder. But historians record that these 400 years were in fact a time of cultural development, and the word 'dark' is more to do with the lack of written history from the period than it is a comment on the prevailing conditions.

dash A decorous expletive lost to English long before the 21st century, but also a useful punctuation mark. Dashes are mainly used either parenthetically (as in brackets) or for dramatic effect or to emphasize a witticism or punchline. Examples are "Liverpool won a famous victory – though not without the help of the one-eyed referee – at Anfield in yesterday's clash" and "the garden bristled with topiary – a place of shear delight."

Typographically, the dash is an en-rule (–) or em-rule (—), a longer mark than a hyphen. In typing, the en-rule is now much more used than the em-rule. Strictly speaking, the en-rule is used to denote a span, as in the London–Paris train, rather than a hyphen. In this use, no spaces are left either side of the rule, but when using the rule as a dash, always leave spaces.

data Information used as the basis for reckoning. Strictly speaking, data is a plural word (singular is datum) so it is correct to write "data are available" rather than "data is … " Latin *datum* (thing given).

dates Which is better: September 11 2001 or 11 September 2001 or 11th September 2001 or September 11th 2001? Some writers include a comma – thus September 11, 2001 and so on. For the sake of brevity, and at no risk to explicitness, dates can safely exclude both the comma and the ordinal denotation, as in 1st, 2nd, 3rd, 4th. Newspapers commonly use the style September 11 2001, but there is a reasonable argument that this can cause confusion due to the proximity of the numerals. The advice that it is helpful to separate the figures with the letters of the month – as in 11 September 2001 – seems reasonable. Note that numerical dates are expressed differently in American and English use. The figures 11/9/01 in British writing denote 11 September 2001, but 9 November 2001 in the US, because Americans put the month before the day.

decimate   Like many words grounded in specific numbers, this one tends to cause differences of opinion. Strictly, to decimate is reduce by a tenth, from the Latin *decimare*, based on *decimus* (ten). But in the 21st century, the word is very commonly used to describe the killing or removal of any large proportion of an army or other group, as in "the blast has decimated the community" or "the workforce has been decimated by redundancies."

decisive   Is it pronounced di SICE iv or di SIZ iv? Lexicographers are not decisive on this point, and most dictionaries offer both forms.

declension   In Latin and subsequently English grammar, the variation in forms of nouns and pronouns according to case (nominative, accusative etc) and number. There is declension of all nouns and pronouns (and adjectives) in Latin but in English, only pronouns, as: I, me, my; we, us, our; he, him, his; they, them, their – and so on.

deconstruction   The analysis of literature by breaking down the text into its component parts. The term describes a legitimate element of scholarship, but has lately taken on pejorative connotations, implying that deconstructing literature will break the spell of the author's inspiration.

decorous   It means proper or dignified, as in behaviour, and has no connection with interior design. Latin *decorus* (seemly).

dénouement   In drama and fiction, the unravelling of the plot towards its conclusion. Write with the accent. French *dénouer* (to untie a knot).

dependant and **dependent**   A dependant is a person, as young children are the dependants in a family. Dependent is an adjective, as young children are dependent on their parents.

de rigueur

de rigueur Dictated by custom, as hats are de rigueur in the royal enclosure at Ascot. Note spelling – with a 'u' after the 'g.' French, meaning 'of strictness.'

derisive and **derisory** In today's English, derisive means mocking or scornful, as a politician's speech met with derisive catcalls. Derisory means contemptibly small or ungenerous, as in a derisory pay offer. Latin *ridere* (to laugh)

derivation The derivation of an English word is usually the earlier language from which we adapted it. Much of English derives from Latin, simply because this was the language of the Romans, who invaded Britain in 55 BC and remained in occupation until the fifth century AD, laying the foundations of our culture. The languages of other invaders have contributed many derivations, too. Anglo-Saxon, Old Norse and Old French are all common sources. Plenty of words have much more modern derivations. There is a continuing process of borrowing or adapting words from contemporary languages, and writers, particularly Shakespeare, are credited with coining hundreds. Most 'new' words are, however, rooted to some extent in ancient languages, even if they sound wholly invented.

desert and **dessert** A desert is a barren landscape. A dessert is a pudding.

despatch See dispatch.

detective story The first fictional detective mystery was probably *The Murders in the Rue Morgue* by American author Edgar Allan Poe, published in 1841. The central figure was French policeman Auguste Dupin, in the original "detective" role. The first character to be described as a "private detective" in fiction is believed to be Bozzle, a retired constable, in Anthony Trollope's *He Knew He was Right*, published in 1869.

deus ex machina In drama and fiction, a literary device in which a hopeless situation is unexpectedly resolved, as if by divine intervention. A fondly remembered example is from the Monty Python film *The Life of Brian*, in which Brian is pursued by Roman soldiers down a dead end street in Nazareth and seems certain to be killed, whereupon he is plucked to safety in a space ship piloted by garrulous aliens. The term is a Latin translation from Greek *theos ek mekhanes* (god from the machine), describing the images of gods suspended above the stage in the dramatic performances of ancient times.

Devil In reference to Satan himself (or herself) use the initial capital. Otherwise, stick to lower case, as in "he (or she) was an old devil."

di- Words that begin with this prefix very often convey a meaning of duality, as in twice, double or in two parts. Form of Greek *dis* (twice).

dia- The countless words beginning with this suffix commonly describe items or actions in which separation or transition can be inferred. Greek *dia* (through).

Di(a)eresis Mark (¨) above a vowel to indicate it has its own sound, as in naïve.

dialect A way of speaking peculiar to a region, as Geordie dialect in north-east England. Also a regional form of a language, identified by non-standard pronunciation, spelling or grammar.

dialectic As a noun, a term from philosophy unrelated to dialect. Beware its use, as dialectic can mean variously the logical examination of the processes of reason (as in the dialectic of a literary work), the investigation of metaphysical contradictions (especially as proposed by German philosophers Hegel and Kant) and in policy considerations, the effects of polarised social interactions. The plural form dialectics is also used.

diallage Remote figure of speech describing the ultimate focusing of originally diverse arguments on single point.

dialogue Conversation between two individuals or two groups, especially in written form.

diction The manner, or choice of words, used in speaking, singing or writing, as in "her diction was impeccable." Latin *dicere* (to say).

dictionary The 21st century was the first to begin with a comprehensive dictionary of English already in existence.

didactic

Although work on the *Oxford English Dictionary* was begun in the 1850s, it was 1928 before the tenth and final volume was published. Earlier English dictionaries had been selective and partial, in the tradition established by Dr Samuel Johnson's two-volume work published in 1755. Dr Johnson's task had been to replicate in the English language a lexicon on the scale of the *Vocabolario* published by the Italian Accademici della Crusca in 1612 as an inventory of all words, past and present, in Italian, with their asserted correct meanings and usages. The Académie Française had followed with its own first French dictionary in 1694. But the Johnson dictionary, though a marvel, was not able to define the language in the way its Italian and French forerunners had done, and the good doctor himself made no pretence that it had. English was already a language evolving too rapidly to be arrested in time by a prescriptive dictionary, and this has remained the case ever since. While the *OED*, which is in a perpetual state of updating, remains the nearest thing we have to a defining source, its off-shoots the Con*cise Oxford* and *Shorter Oxford* appear regularly in new editions, supplemented by volumes such as the *Oxford Dictionary of New Words*. Other major publishers of English dictionaries are Chambers and Collins.

didactic   It simply means instructive or of use in teaching, but is now much used to suggest a manner of teaching or communication that is pedantic or intellectually intolerant. Avoid didactic in this sense. If you mean pedantic, say pedantic. The fancy term autodidact, incidentally, means a self-taught person, not an authoritarian teacher. From Greek *didaktikos*.

dieresis   See diaerisis.

different   Which is correct: different to, or different from, as in 'his views were different to/from hers'? The latter was once widely considered the only acceptable usage, but both are now just about equally employed. 'Different than' should always be avoided.

digest   A shortened version as, most famously, in *Reader's Digest*. Curiously, the noun is pronounced DYE jest and the verb di JEST.

diminutive   A word form indicating smallness, as a maisonette, a home comprising part of a larger house, is a diminutive of a maison (French for house).

dis-   The prefix denoting either a negative, a splitting into two, or a removal seems to be used to create numerous new words every year. But oddities such as disbenefit and discommend, much in use in the 21st century, appeared in dictionaries long before this century.

disbelief, suspension of   Now a cliché, but the vital conspiracy between authors and their customers. Readers and audiences must be willing to suspend their disbelief if they are to enjoy fiction or drama to the full, all the while knowing really that it's all made up. Writers in their turn must produce work that makes the suspension of disbelief the easiest of tasks.

disc and **disk**   Although the spelling disk has been imported into British English with American computer terminology – as in diskette and disk drive – the spelling disc persists in anatomy ("slipped disc") and even in compact disc and disc jockey.

discourse   The noun can mean both a two-way conversation and a monologue. The verb means only to talk or write in a learned way.

discreet and **discrete**   Discreet means tactful or circumspect. Discrete means distinct or separate.

discursive   Polite word for rambling, as a kindly tutor might say a student who has wandered from the point in an essay has been discursive, rather than merely irrelevant. In philosophy, discursive means following a rational argument from premise to conclusion, as in a discourse.

dispatch   Use this spelling, and not the pointless variation despatch.

diss   Short for disrespect, a recent slang word now usually used as a verb, as in "Don't you diss me." Original informal spelling may have been 'dis.'

dissemble   It means to deceive by concealing one's true motives or feelings, as in "she dissembled beautifully when asked her opinion of the appalling portrait." For taking things apart, use disassemble.

distil

distil One 'l' for the verb but two for all its forms, as distillery, distilling.

divers and **diverse** Divers is now falling out of use, but has never been strictly synonymous with diverse. Divers means several or sundry, as in "divers reports" and diverse means dissimilar or varied, as in "diverse views."

doctor The connection of this word to medicine is quite recent. It is Latin for 'one who instructs' from the verb *docere*, to teach. In Britain, the universal abbreviation Dr usually denotes a medical practitioner. In the United States, the title holder may equally be practising medicine, veterinary medicine or dentistry. The title doctor was originally conferred by universities on graduates in many different disciplines who achieved the highest degree available, a doctorate, commonly called a PhD – *Philosophiae Doctor* (Doctor of Philosophy). Holders of such degrees from recognised institutions continue to have the same right as medical professionals to call themselves 'doctor.' Many members of the clergy are holders of doctorates in divinity (initials DD).

doggerel Informal term for bad or facetious poetry.

dog's bollocks English idiom of the 1920s first coined as a superlative along with many other animal images including 'cat's pyjamas' and 'ant's pants.' The expression did not catch on in its early life, but entered the 21st century as a distressingly common term, as in "he thinks he's the dog's bollocks on the soccer field," or "that film was the dog's bollocks."

domestic As a noun, it came originally into use by police for an altercation in a private household to which they were called by one of the participants. A domestic is now more widely taken to be any kind of domestic dispute – inside or outside the home. Latin *domus* (house).

double entendre Although obsolete in French, this curious borrowing is still in common use in English, and French pronunciation persists, approximately, as 'dooble on TAWN druh.' Originally meaning 'double understanding' it is a word or phrase to which at least two interpretations could be attributed, one of them usually mildly obscene. A device very much favoured by comedians.

draft and **draught**   Here is a phrase from the first sentence of an article about shopping for books in Britain in *The Daily Telegraph* of 13 December 2003: "An elderly woman breaks from the street-shoal of Christmas shoppers to stand blinking in the fluorescent light of Waterstone's drafty foyer."

There is no word 'drafty' in the English language. What the writer meant was 'draughty.' The spelling draft is used only to convey the sense of something drawn, as in a money order, a sketch or manuscript, or (historically) conscription for military service in the US. Otherwise, the word is draught, as in the current of air, quantity of liquid, disc for playing the game draughts, and so on.

drama   In literature, a play written for performance in a theatre or for broadcast. The art originated in ancient Greece and the word is ancient Greek for 'action.'

dramatis personae   The cast of characters in a play. Latin for 'the persons of the drama.'

Dubya   One of the first new words of the 21st century. It refers to the initial W in the name of US President George Walker Bush Jnr, and mocks the President's pronunciation of the letter. Now, the word is showing signs of adoption as a general term of abuse for non-metropolitan politicians with right-of-centre leanings.

dysphemism   Figure of speech emphasizing the unpleasant, especially in a familiar phrase altered via the substitution of a key word, as in "a diplomat sent abroad to lie for his country." The opposite of euphemism.

E

Earth When writing of our own planet in the context of the solar system, use the initial capital and not the definite article, as in Jupiter, Mars, Earth etc.

echoic Describes a type of word that imitates a sound, as in crunch, splat or thwack. Similar to onomatopeic (*qv*).

eclectic Enduring buzz word arises from philosophical practice of plucking ideas from a variety of sources rather than from one particular school of thought. Now used to mean any wide-ranging set of tastes or ideas. Greek *eklego* (to pick out).

eclogue A short poem. Greek *eklego* (to pick out).

eco- The prefix denoting ecology is sometimes hyphenated, sometimes not. Current conventions include: eco-friendly, ecosphere, ecosystem, eco-terrorism, ecotourist, eco-warrior.

e-commerce Business conducted via the Internet.

ecstasy Besides the sense of overwhelming rapture, an illegal drug. In the 21st century it is now common to write the name of the drug (methylenedioxymethamphetamine) without an initial capital. Greek *ekstasis* (standing outside the self).

ectoplasm If this curious but widespread word means anything, it is the outer layer of the part of a cell known as the cytoplasm. But ectoplasm has been adopted in the world of the occult for a mysterious exudation said to flow from the body of medium during communication with 'the other side.' Greek *ektos* (outside) and *plasso* (to shape).

educationalist and **educationist** The two terms are synonymous and refer to someone expert in teaching methods, and who promotes the merits of education.

Edwardian A brief period of distinctive British architecture and fashion. Refers to the reign of King Edward VII from 1901 to 1910.

eerie and **eyrie** Eerie is an adjective meaning strange or frightening. An eyrie is an eagle's nest or, metaphorically, any inaccessible retreat built in a high place.

Eeyore Fictional stereotype from A A Milne's *Winnie the Pooh*. A toy donkey, Eeyore is perpetually pessimistic – the antithesis of another character from the story, and similarly enduring fictional stereotype, the persistently cheerful Tigger.

effect See affect.

effects Belongings, as in "He was given permission to collect his effects." There is no such noun as affects.

egregious Jocular buzz word means outstandingly bad, as in "it was an egregious performance even by the low standards of this entertainer." Oddly enough, the word meant outstandingly able or meritorious until recent times. Latin *ex* (out of) and *grex* (flock).

elegy A song or poem of lament, often for the dead. Greek *elegos* (mourning verse).

elision Running two words together and abbreviating to form a single word, as in 'mustn't' from 'must not' or 'they've' from 'they have.'

elite It is now common to write it without the accent (élite), but the word is pronounced in the French manner, 'eh LEET'.

Elizabethan This still refers principally to the reign of English monarch Elizabeth I (1558–1603).

ellipsis The leaving out of a word, as in "(it) seems fine to me" or "I have to go and (to) get more money." When showing an ellipsis with punctuation to indicate a break in a quotation or other text, type the three stops with spaces either side, as "one, two ... eight, nine."

em An old printer's measurement, so-called after the width of a capital 'M' and standardised at about 4.2 millimetres. An em-rule (—) is a punctuation form – in effect a dash – that has now fallen into disuse. It has been replaced by the en-rule, so-called because it is exactly half the length.

email English

email English The brevity vital to text messages sent between mobile telephones and palm-top computers has bred a shorthand of its own, in which keypad numbers figure significantly. 'To' is consequently keyed as 2, 'for' as 4 and so on. Single letters are adopted on a phonetic basis as substitutes for words – n for 'and', r for 'are' etc. Some keyboard symbols, known as 'smileys' or 'emoticons' are adopted to convey emotion. Thus :-(the keystrokes for ☹ placed at the end of a message express sympathy. E-mail English is set to develop its own considerable vocabulary – to the dismay of some educationists, who warn that literacy may be the loser. See also text message and txt.

emoticon Computerese word for the 'smiley' messages used in text messaging and email. See email English. From back formation 'emote' from emotion.

empathy and **sympathy** Somehow, empathy appears to be blending with sympathy as a word to describe feelings of pity or compassion for someone who is suffering. Sympathy is probably a victim of political correctness, deemed patronising in a world where sufferers receive medical treatment, counselling or 'care' from paid professionals rather than mere love and kindness from friends (as distinct from family). But writers need to beware substitution, because while sympathy comes to us from ancient Greek – *sun* (with) and *pathos* (feeling) – empathy is a word coined as recently as 1904 as a translation for German *Einfühlung*, meaning mutual understanding or like-mindedness. Empathy is a sentiment more selfish and detached than sympathy.

emphasis Additional stress given to a word by raising the voice or, in written text, underlining or italicising, as in "I really *hate* that man."

empirical Beware confusion with the adjective 'imperial' from empire. Empirical means based on experience or observation rather than on more scientific principles, from Greek *empeira* (experience).

en-rule Punctuation form better known as a dash. An en is an old printer's measurement, defined as half an 'em' (*qv*).

enantiosis   Part of speech expressing the quality of something via a negative of its opposite, as in something good described as 'not bad.'

encomium   Speech or text in praise of a person, object, event or idea. Plural is encomiums.

England   Distinct nation within the realm known variously as Britain, British Isles, Great Britain or United Kingdom. While it might be common for Americans to describe the entirety of the realm as 'England,' none of the nation's subjects should dare to do so.

English   The word describes the population of the nation of England – about 50 million at the beginning of the 21st century – and the first language of about 500 million people worldwide. The word derives from the Latin *Anglus*, describing a tribe from Schleswig (now in northern Germany) who first settled in eastern England in the 5th century AD.

enquiry and **inquiry**   As a rule, use enquiry for informal questioning or investigation, as in "she made enquiries about employment," and inquiry for more official business, as "a police inquiry." The same goes for the verbs enquire and inquire.

enrol   Note spelling in British English. To enroll is to join up in American English.

ensure and **insure**   To ensure is to make certain, as in "he ensured she had her keys with her." To insure is to protect against possible loss, as in "she insured her life."

envelope   Originally a French word meaning 'bundle' this item of stationery is now commonly heard in the idiom 'pushing the envelope.' It derives from the jargon of the United States Air Force. Pilots refer to the official speed and manoeuvre limitations of their aircraft as 'the envelope' and the practice of flying beyond those design limits as pushing it. The phrase has now been adapted for any practice – such as in sport or business-risk-taking – in which activities are undertaken beyond the usually accepted limits, as in "we're really going to push the envelope in this sales campaign." Note the spelling, without a final 'e,' of the

epic

verb 'to envelop' and that the first syllable is pronounced 'EN' and no longer as in the French 'ON.'

epic Once upon a time it meant a lengthy, heroic poem such as the *Iliad* of Homer, or John Milton's *Paradise Lost*, centred on great legends or other beliefs. But now the word is much more widely applied, to blockbuster films or historical novels. Even sporting events such as soccer matches are commonly described as "epic encounters." Greek *epos* (song).

epigram A witty saying or motto, often as a short rhyme, as in Ogden Nash's immortal "Candy is dandy, but liquor is quicker."

epigraph Words inscribed on a statue, official building, coin or medal, as in "In God We Trust" or "For Valour."

epilogue The afterword in a play or book.

epiphany The Epiphany, in Christian scripture, is the day on which the infant Jesus was shown to the pagans – symbolised by the Three Kings or Magi – on a date now held to be 6 January. This date was once Christmas Day, but is now the last day of the Christmas festival, Twelfth Night. It is curious that in an increasingly secular world, the word epiphany has now come into very wide general use. In its original sense, from the Greek *epiphainein*, to reveal, via Old French usage, it means a great, life-changing revelation. But 21st-century writers in English commonly use it to denote any kind of influential event, as in "a day of epiphanies."

episode In drama and fiction, a segment of a story, but also any distinct event in a narrative, as 'a shocking episode.'

epistolary In the form of letters. The earliest modern novels in the English language were commonly epistolary, such as Samuel Richardson's *Pamela* and *Clarissa Harlowe*, in which the stories are revealed in exchanges of letters between the protagonists and their confidantes. Greek *epistello* (to send news).

epitaph The words inscribed on a tomb, or the motto by which an individual would like to be remembered after their death. Comedian Spike Milligan (1918–2002) insisted on "I told you I was ill."

epithet An adjective appended to the name of an individual, identifying the characteristic for which they are known, as in Peter the Great, or Ivan the Terrible.

epizeuxis Part of speech in which a word is repeated for emphasis, as in "that is so, so not funny."

eponym A word owing its origin to the name of a person, real or imaginary. Also, the person after whom a story or drama is named. Thus, the Simpsons are the eponym of the central family of characters of the US television series of the same name and the Simpsons themselves are the eponymous heroes. There are many useful eponyms in common usage, including the following selection:

ampere – an electrical unit, after French scientist André Marie Ampère.

atlas – book of maps, after Atlas, a Titan of Greek mythology taxed with carrying the weight of the whole world on his shoulders.

Biro – a trademarked type of ballpoint pen patented by Hungarian Lászlo Biró.

bloomers – outdated feminine underwear introduced by American Amelia Bloomer.

bowdlerize – to edit written work indiscriminately, after English doctor Thomas Bowdler.

boycott – to shun contact with or refuse any dealings with, after Irish landlord Captain Charles Boycott.

Braille – reading system for the blind devised by French inventor Louis Braille.

cardigan – woollen garment fastened with buttons, after the Earl of Cardigan.

chauvinist – single-minded patriot, after French politician Nicolas Chauvin.

derrick – type of crane, often shipboard, after 17th-century hangman named Derrick.

diesel – type of combustion engine and the fuel it burns, after German engineer Rudolf Diesel.

draconian – harsh style of administration, after Athenian ruler Draco, 7th century BC.

dunce – person of low intelligence, after Duns Scotus, medieval Scottish teacher.

galvanise – to provoke into sudden action, after metal process devised by Italian Luigi Galvani.

guillotine – to cut off, or a device for cutting, after instrument of decapitation credited to French doctor Joseph Ignace Guillotin.

hoover – to use a vacuum cleaner, after William Henry Hoover, US manufacturer.

leotard – one-piece costume of dancers and athletes, after French acrobat Jules Léotard.

luddite – a person destructively disposed to technological advancement, after English farm labourer and machine smasher Ned Ludd.

mackintosh – waterproof outer garment, after Scottish chemist Charles Macintosh.

malapropism – the muddling of words to comic effect, after Mrs Malaprop, a character created by English dramatist Richard Sheridan in *The Rivals*.

martinet – a fastidious, cruel ruler or commander, after French army officer Jean Martinet.

masochist – person who derives sexual pleasure from cruel treatment, after German novelist Sacher-Maso.

maverick – an independent-minded person, after American adventurer Samuel Maverick.

mesmerise – to hypnotise or hold in thrall, after German doctor Franz Mesmer.

Micawber – lovable, well-intentioned but feckless spendthrift, after the character in Charles Dickens's *David Copperfield*.

narcissist – an excessively vain person, after self-admiring Narcissus of Greek mythology.

pasteurise – to sterilise by heating, after French scientist Louis Pasteur.

pavlova – meringue-based dessert, named in honour of Russian ballerina Anna Pavlova.

platonic – in matters of love, a relationship confined to an intellectual and/or spiritual dimension, after Greek philosopher Plato.

promethean – of a boldly innovative person or idea, after Greek mythological character Prometheus, who stole fire from the gods.

pyrrhic – in conflict, a victory won at too high a cost, after Pyrrhus, an ancient king of Epirus, who defeated the Romans at Heraclea in 280BC and proclaimed "Another victory like this and we lose the war."

quisling – a traitor, after Norwegian Vidkun Quisling, premier who collaborated with the Nazis in the Second World War.

sadist – practitioner of sadism, the inflicting of cruelty for pleasure, after French writer and pervert the Marquis de Sade.

salmonella – bacteria causing food poisoning, after American veterinary surgeon Daniel E Salmon.

sandwich – a meal of any type of ingredients placed between slices of bread, said to have been the invention of a gambling-addicted Earl of Sandwich who did not wish to rise from the gaming table to eat.

shrapnel – fragments of an explosive shell, after a shell filled with musketballs devised by English soldier Henry Shrapnel.

Shylock – malignantly acquisitive person, after Jewish villain of Shakespeare's *The Merchant of Venice*.

silhouette – outline of a shape, usually the human face or figure, after French statesman Etienne de Silhouette.

simony – the sale of church livings, after biblical Simon Magnus, a first-century confidence trickster.

spoonerism – the muddling of letters within or among words, after English academic Rev W A Spooner.

tantalise – to torment by offering, then withdrawing, goods or favours, after Tantalus of Greek mythology, punished in this way by Zeus.

Uriah Heep – an obsequious but untrustworthy person, after villain of Charles Dickens's *David Copperfield*.

volt – unit of electrical force, after Italian scientist Alessandro Volta.

watt – unit of power, after Scottish steam engineer James Watt.

-er and **-or**   These two suffixes, signifying agency – a person or object with a function – cause endless trouble. Which is correct: adviser or advisor, protester or protestor? There are many such words dictionaries refuse to rule on, blandly stating both spellings. There is no answer except to be consistent. As a rule, a word that ends only in -or – actor, prosecutor, tractor, victor – will have derived directly from Latin. Words ending exclusively with -er have mostly come down via Middle or Old English – angler, harvester, killer, printer.

erotic   Now used to describe anything stimulating sexual desire, it was once little more than a synonym for romantic. From Greek god of love Eros, who in later mythology became a mischievous child.

-ess   The suffix denoting femaleness has barely survived into the 21st century. Few but the longest-established words, such as duchess and princess, imported from French, are any longer in widely accepted use. Gender-specific terms such as air hostess and stewardess have been displaced by attendant. Actress is gradually giving way to actor; authoress, manageress and murderess are already extinct. Those that linger, presumably for utter lack of neutral alternatives, include waitress and, oddly, temptress.

essay   A written composition. The word comes from the earlier English 'assay' meaning to weigh.

Establishment   A notional elite in ownership and control of a nation. The British 'Establishment' (in this context it is customarily written with an initial capital to convey a sense of permanence) is said to have been the invention of writer Henry Fairlie in an article for the political weekly *The Spectator* in 1955.

Estuary English   Late 20th-century term for accented language originally associated with the Cockney of London, but now applying to a wider span of southeast England, particularly in the estuarial reaches of the River Thames, notably the county of Essex. Use of Estuary English proliferates via film, radio and television, because many popular actors, presenters and interviewees from the region – which is culturally dominant in the UK – speak in this way and are imitated by admiring viewers and listeners throughout the country. This form of English, earlier known as 'Mockney' – Cockney adopted by people living outside the Cockney homeland of east London – is predicted to become the new 'received pronunciation' nationwide.

-et Regular verbs with two or more syllables ending in -et can present problems in conjugation (*qv*). In the perfect tense, for example, abet becomes abetted, but target becomes targeted. Why the double 't' for one but not for the other? As a rule it's a matter of phonetics. In the word abet, the stress is on the second syllable, so the perfect form takes the double 't.' In target, the stress is on the first syllable, thus one 't.' All single-syllable verbs – bet, fret, set, vet etc – with the -et ending take the double 't' form.

e-tail Recent term for selling goods and services via the internet.

etc Abbreviation of Latin *et cetera* (and more of the same) can now safely be written without a full point.

etymology The derivation and evolution of words. Greek *etumon* (true). Beware confusion with entomology, the study of insects.

eulogy A spoken or written address in praise of an individual, most usually in the form of funeral oration.

euphemism Figure of speech. A description that seeks to camouflage or to improve on an unpleasant truth. Examples are a violent fist fight reported as 'a bit of a dust-up' and civilian casualties dismissed by military spokesmen as 'collateral damage.' Euphemism may be used to confer an imagined legitimacy or social acceptability on the activities of particular groups. Drug addicts and their apologists speak of 'doing' heroin rather than the balder 'injecting' it.

   In the context of political correctness, euphemism has proliferated. Public health and welfare services have developed whole new vocabularies in their struggle to appear unbiased in any way in dealings with 'clients' (patients are rarely mentioned). Deaf becomes aurally impaired (replacing insufficiently euphemistic hard of hearing) and visually impaired replaces blind; the mentally ill have learning difficulties and the poor are 'C2s' (referring to a scale used by the advertising industry to define the earning power and social standing of target audiences).

euro

Euphemism has long been a device of popular drama and literature. Gangsters in thriller fiction 'eliminate', 'rub out' or 'waste' their victims, rather than killing them. In a memorable military briefing in the 1979 film *Apocalypse Now*, the hero is instructed to murder a senior fellow officer by 'terminating his command with extreme prejudice.' No topic attracts as many euphemisms as dying – from Shakespeare's 'shuffled off this mortal coil' (Hamlet 2i) to the pious 'passed away' and robust 'flatlined' of more modern times.

euro Write the currency unit all in lower case, as for sterling and the dollar.

exclamation mark Item of punctuation (!) deserving the most judicious use. American author Mark Twain said a writer placing an exclamation mark at the end of a sentence was, in effect, laughing at his own joke. A subsequent American author, F Scott Fitzgerald, said just the same. English writer Lynne Truss, whose book *Eats, Shoots & Leaves: the Zero Tolerance Approach to Punctuation* (Profile Books) became a surprise bestseller in 2003, developed the theme admirably by saying: "I can attest that there is only one thing more mortifying than having an exclamation mark removed by an editor: having an exclamation mark added." Certainly the use of exclamation marks in any but the most-practised hands tends to denote naïvety in the writer. But in some cases, the mark is vital to indicate the urgency of a command or appeal for attention. 'Help' and 'Help!' are clearly distinct. In 21st-century writing – from private letters to newspaper headlines – the mark is used more often to denote jocularity or irony than to give emphasis.

exegesis Buzz word among the loftier literati for the critical analysis of a written work. It was once confined to interpretations of scripture, and should probably continue in that limited role. Greek for 'interpretation.'

existential Whatever does this word, as in phrases such as "I've just had an existential experience," really mean? The origin is in the school of philosophy known as Existentialism, which arises in Europe in the first half of the 19th century. The proposition was that man, rather than God, is at the centre of existence. It was only after the Second World War that Existentialism became familiar outside the cloistered world of the philosophers, when the atheist French writer Jean Paul Sartre produced plays and novels exploring his own humanist version of the doctrine, influenced by the experience of the Nazi occupation of France. Earlier philosophers associated with the Existentialist movement include the German Georg Hegel and Dane Søren Kierkegaard, but Sartre's beliefs and teachings were distinct. Because of the diversity of thought encompassed by the generic term existentialist, it is probably unwise to use the word outside the specific contexts of the various philosophical movements connected with it. But contemporary writers find it difficult to resist, as in this opaque passage by Jeremy Clarke in *The Spectator* in 2002: "Half a morning on the phone talking to robotic phone operators in anonymous call centres had made me feel existentially alienated, frightened even."

expatriate   A person living abroad. Beware common misspelling 'expatriot.'

explicit   Now mostly used to describe a narrative in which sexuality is frankly portrayed. But the word has the wider meaning of clearly stated or explained, as in "she described his shortcomings in explicit detail." The opposite of implicit, in which meaning is taken to be understood without overt statement.

exponential   Buzz word. An exponent in mathematics is the power by which any given number can be raised, so that in '3 squared' (3 times 3, or 3^2) = 9, the exponent is 2. This has given rise to the adjective exponential, which the Oxford dictionaries say describes an increase that "becomes more and more rapid." In this sense, exponential is a mere synonym for accelerating.

exposition   In a story, the first part, setting the scene and introducing characters.

Expressionism   Writers and artists subscribing to this school of thought are endeavouring to communicate their own emotions through their work, rather than objectively depicting the external world.

eyesore   One word.

F

fable A story, often with a moral, as in *Aesop's Fables*. It is the source of the word fabulous, which once consequently meant something imagined, legendary or absurd. Now, fabulous is more likely to describe something excellent or wonderful. Use 'fabled' for the older meaning.

factious and **fractious** Factious means behaving according to the tenets of a faction or minority group, as in "the factious views of the party's extreme right-wing." Fractious means behaving in an irritable or peevish manner, as in "fractious exchanges between political opponents."

faithfully The sign-off in formal letters addressed to a recipient not identified by name. If your letter has to start with Dear Sir or Dear Madam, it should end with Yours faithfully.

falling-out A disagreement. Write with a hyphen.

fallout Radioactive aftermath. Write as one word.

false friends An informal term in linguistics for identical or similar-sounding words in different languages which have diverse meanings. At the simplest level there can be trivial confusion between everyday words such as French *carte* (card, menu etc) and English cart or German *aktuell* (at present) and English actual. But more problematic conflicts of meaning arise with trade names. America's General Motors had to find a new name for their Vauxhall Nova car in Spain when it was discovered that *no va* in Spanish means 'doesn't go.'

farce Originally, an absurd type of comedy, and now any absurd unfolding of events. Latin *farcire*, meaning to stuff – and thus to fill unoccupied time with something of trivial value.

farther or **further** As the comparative form of 'far' farther is a latecomer. Further was the original extension in Old English, with farther a "mere variant" according to the *OED*, first recorded as late as 1460. Farther came into use to distinguish the comparative of far, in the sense of 'at a greater distance' from the many other meanings acquired by further – as adjective, adverb and verb – but is now not much used. The same fate has befallen farthest.

fat cat A wealthy businessman or latterly an official, particularly one perceived to be overpaid. The term arises from China's Cultural Revolution of 1966 when any person with noticeable wealth was likely to be branded with the name – a traditional Chinese insult – and accordingly punished. Hongkong Chinese millionaires, safe in what was then a British Crown colony, were then proud to be called fat cats in defiance of the communist regime across the border, and the term thence spread around the world.

FD Recent term of abuse among teenagers stands for Fashion Disaster. Young people not conforming to current designer-label dress code may find themselves thus addressed.

feint A feigned attack or a diversion to fool an attacker. Not related to faint.

feminine The word is not always interchangeable with female. In grammar, there are words of feminine, not female, gender. Animals are never feminine. While female distinguishes women from men, feminine has implications of womanliness. Latin *femina* (woman).

feminism The doctrine of asserting the rights of women to equality with men in every sphere of life.

ferment and **foment** To ferment means principally to cause sugars to turn to alcohol in a tumultuous process stimulated by the presence of yeast. The process itself is called a ferment or fermentation. But a ferment can also be a more metaphorical tumult, as "the team was in a ferment of anxiety before the match." The verb to foment is distinct, meaning to stir up, as in 'to foment a rebellion.'

fewer and **less** These two words need to be kept for separate occasions. When describing a smaller number of items – whether abstract, animal, vegetable or mineral – use fewer, as in "there are fewer jobs on offer than there were in my young days," or "fewer customers turned up than had been expected," or "this restaurant has fewer tables than the one next door." Use the word less only when describing a smaller quantity on something that cannot be enumerated – again whether abstract, animal, vegetable or mineral – as in, "there is less time left than I had thought," or "he's less of a man than he used to be," or "there's less marmalade than I need."

fey This ancient and beautiful Old English word should only be used in its original sense of close to death, or possessed by the delirious elation said to be felt in the moment before dying. But it is now used in a woolly way to describe various conditions of being other-worldly or even fairy-like. These recently acquired associations are due to confusion with the unrelated word fay, meaning a fairy.

fiancé Write with the accent and in the French feminine form fiancée where the intended is to be the bride.

fiction An imaginary work, usually a novel or short story. Publishing divides its activities between fiction and non-fiction.

fictional stereotypes Some distinctively drawn characters from drama and fiction have been adopted to exemplify types of people in the 'real' world. Writers past and present may presume too much, however, on the literary knowledge of their readers. For example, while most of us know a 'Romeo' is a young man with a fond eye, from Shakespeare's *Romeo & Juliet*, do so many of us know that a 'Svengali' is a person who exerts overwhelming manipulative power over another, after an evil hypnotist in a forgotten novel called *Trilby* written by George du Maurier?

Following are some common fictional stereotypes and their origins:

Bluebeard – a man who preys on women, particularly one who marries, then murders, his brides in succession. From *La Barbe Bleue* (*Blue Beard*), a fairy tale by Charles Perrault (1628–1703).
Cinderella – a girl, or more recently any item or concept, unfairly

overlooked and sometimes ultimately redeemed. From *Cendrillon ou la petite pantoufle de verre* (*Cinderella or the little glass slipper*), a fairy tale by Charles Perrault.

Faustian – of a person who has exchanged honour and self-respect for material gain, or of such an exchange itself, as in a Faustian pact. From the story of a disillusioned German conjurer who traded his soul for immortality in a pact with the Devil. There are two great versions of the tale, *Dr Faustus* by Christopher Marlowe in 1604, and *Faust* by Goethe, who is said to have begun the work in 1770 and not completed it until 1832.

Dorian Gray – a man who seems never to age, but whose eternal youth may owe itself to some sinister secret. From Oscar Wilde's only novel, *The Picture of Dorian Gray* (1891).

Jekyll and Hyde – a person whose behaviour alternates between normal and abnormal or good and bad. From *The Strange Case of Dr Jekyll and Mr Hyde* by R L Stevenson (1886).

John Bull – typical Englishman, after John Arbuthnot's *History of John Bull* (1712).

Micawber – someone cheerfully hopeless with money who always expects to come into cash at any moment, after Wilkins Micawber in *David Copperfield* by Charles Dickens (1849–50).

Walter Mitty – a fantasist, especially an underachiever who imagines great success and becomes entrapped by false boasting. From *The Secret Life of Walter Mitty* (1946) by James Thurber.

Panglossian – holding ridiculously optimistic views about the state of the world, from Dr Pangloss in Voltaire's philosophical tale *Candide* (1859).

Peter Pan – a boy who never grows up. From *Peter Pan* by J M Barrie (1904).

quixotic – of a person whose behaviour is absurdly chivalrous or idealistic. From *Don Quixote* (1605) by Miguel de Cervantes.

pollyanna – an incipiently optimistic person, from *Pollyanna*, a novel by Eleanor Hodgman Porter (1868–1920).

Scrooge – a miser, from Ebenezer Scrooge in *A Christmas Carol* by Charles Dickens (1843).

Shylock – abusive term for any miserly or greedy person, especially Jewish. From *The Merchant of Venice* (1596) by William Shakespeare.

Uncle Tom – a black man submissive to whites. From *Uncle Tom's Cabin* by Harriet Beecher Stowe (1852).

figure of speech   In the use of language, a device that heightens the impact of what is said or written, as in a metaphor used to create a picture or sensation in words, such as "the wine-dark sea."

first person   The first person singular is 'I' and the first person plural is 'we.'

First World War   In British English, this is still more commonly used than the mainly American World War One (or I). Some publications have very recently begun to do without the initial capitals.

flair and **flare**   Flair is an instinct, as in "she has a flair for colour coordination." Flare, as a noun, means variously a bright light, a widening of material in tailoring or an outward curve.

flak   Originally the explosive blast from anti-aircraft shells, this word has now come to mean heated criticism or dissent, as in "he caught a lot of flak after missing the penalty." Note the spelling (no 'c'), which is a contraction of German *Flugabwehrkanone*, an anti-aircraft gun.

flare   See flair.

flatline   Recent unpleasant euphemism meaning to die. It derives from hospital use of vital-systems monitors displaying a graphic representation of the heartbeat. When the patient dies the oscillating line subsides to a flat line.

flier   See flyer.

flyer   Even though the verb conjugates 'I fly, you fly, he flies,' a person who flies is spelled flyer – although flier is given as an alternative in dictionaries.

fly-on-the-wall   Voyeuristic or secretly observed, as in a fly-on-the-wall documentary. Use the hyphens.

foment   See ferment.

font   In printing, a typeface. From Latin *fundere*, to pour, the word recalls the era of 'hot-metal' typesetting when molten lead was poured into type moulds.

Fools rush in where angels fear to tread   Enduring aphorism was written by Alexander Pope in his *Essay on Criticism* in 1711.

for- or **fore-**   Many words begin with the prefix for(e)-, which indicates a sense of before (in time) or in front of (in place). But there are variations in spelling which can be confusing. There is some logic involved, as many words prefixed with for- take this form because they derive from Old English, signifying distance, counteraction, intensiveness, destruction or exhaustion – as in forbid and forsake. But most words in this big group take the prefix with the 'e' as in forearm, forecast and foresee. To add to the confusion, some of these words are now listed in dictionaries as having acceptable alternative spellings, such as for(e)bear, for(e)go and for(e)warn. The easiest method of getting these words right is to remember that only a few start exclusively with the prefix for-. They are as follows:

forbear	forfend	forlorn
forbid	forget	forsake
forfeit	forgive	fortify
		forward

forensic   It means judicial, as in the kind of open-air law court of Ancient Rome called a *forum*. Now used almost exclusively in the context of medicine and science, where police seek to find 'forensic evidence' in support of prosecutions.

forever and **for ever**   These are distinct adverbs, Forever means continually or repeatedly, as in "she is forever complaining." For ever means for all time, as in "only two things are for ever – death and taxes."

foreword   Preface to a book. Beware confusion with 'forward.'

founder The verb means to collapse or sink. Avoid confusion with flounder, meaning to struggle helplessly or desperately, as in muddled thought or speech – or even in drowning. Latin *fundus* (bottom).

fraught

fraught   Strictly speaking, it means loaded (as in freight) or filled, as in the phrase 'fraught with danger.' But the word has now evolved, informally, to the point where it is used alone to convey the sense of words it once merely qualified, as in 'things got a bit fraught.' Avoid this, for the moment, in formal writing. From Old Dutch *vracht* (freight).

free verse   Poetry in which the conventions of metre, rhythm and rhyme are disregarded. Cynics might say this kind of verse now accounts for all poetry, but the form has been around a long time. Consider this verse from a poem by John Keats, written about 200 years ago:

> There was a naughty Boy,
> A naughty boy was he,
> He would not stop at home,
> He could not quiet be –
> He took
> In his Knapsack
> A Book
> Full of vowels
> And a shirt
> With some towels –
> A slight cap
> For night cap –
> A hair brush,
> Comb ditto,
> New Stockings
> For old ones
> Would split O!
> This Knapsack
> Tight at's back
> He rivetted close
> And followed his Nose
> To the North,
> To the North,
> And follow'd his nose
> To the North.

French – borrowings from Countless words in English have joined the language from French, particularly since the Norman Conquest, and the process continues to this day. Words that have naturalised, such as hotel and place, are indistinguishable from indigenous English. But more recent arrivals that still look foreign can present problems. Should phrases such as 'de trop' (unwanted) and 'de rigueur' (compulsory) be written in quote marks or typed in italics to acknowledge their foreignness? The answer is no. These phrases may be French, but they have dual nationality. They can safely be treated as English. The same goes for the many products from France that are now familiar exports, from camembert to cassoulet, from cabriolet to chaise-longue. The only French words or phrases that need be qualified by quote marks or italicisation are those that remain unfamiliar in what might be called mainstream or everyday English. Examples are *bien pensant* (right thinking) and *folie de jeunesse* (foolishness of youth). It's a reasonable rule that if such words or phrases are not included in a concise dictionary, they can be regarded as sufficiently foreign to italicise or write in quote marks.

Where words are recognisably French, write them as they are written in French, with their correct accents, as in château, cliché and déjà vu.

full stop Also called full point or period (US), it's the punctuation mark placed at the end of a sentence or marking the end of an abbreviated word. Its use to punctuate initials has eroded rapidly in recent years, so that it is now quite unusual to write Mr., U.K. and so on. It is an axiom of good, clear writing that maximum use is made of the full stop. Short, concise, complete sentences punctuated with full stops are invariably preferable to long sentences stretched with commas or conjunctions, complicated by subordinate clauses or ineptly compartmented with semicolons. Note to writers: The previous sentence is a good example of an unnecessarily long sentence.

Should full stops ever be placed outside quotation marks? Strictly speaking, where a quotation or reported speech do not form the entirety of the sentence, there is a case for punctuating as

fulsome

follows: She turned from the window and said "good morning". But the detached full stop looks odd, and there are plenty of writers and editors who make a habit of tucking it within the quote marks, just for tidiness. The author of this book freely confesses to being of their number.

fulsome   The author of this book confesses to using this word with deplorable regularity in his writings on the subject of wine. I continue to do so, but have been upbraided by one reader who wrote to say: "Will you forgive me if I pick you up on one word that you often use to describe, I would guess, a certain roundness and body in a wine? This is 'fulsome' which I don't think has anything to do with 'full-bodied.' My dictionary says: fulsome adj. excessive or insincere, esp. in an offensive or distasteful way e.g. fulsome compliments. I don't think any decent wine would merit that adjective." I replied: "Congratulations on your sharp eye for the weasel word. My use of fulsome is misleading, but my excuse is that I am using it out of time. By which I mean that the Middle English word, as used until the 1600s in its original sense, meant 'abundant and plentiful' and even, according to the *Shorter Oxford Dictionary*, 'full and plump, fat, well-grown.' Like so many adjectives that once delineated fleshly delights, fulsome has gradually accumulated pejorative significance. Shakespeare uses the word to convey corruption and lustfulness, and Francis Bacon thinks it means malodorous."

fun   Once a mere noun, fun has been extended into use as an adjective – "we had a fun time" – and more lately as an intransitive verb – "we're going out to fun." This is nothing more than a revival of a much earlier use of fun, meaning to make sport, that had hitherto been obsolete for several centuries.

functional literacy   Phrase used by educationists to describe an acceptable level of reading and writing ability as measured in British children aged 11, the stage at which they move from primary to secondary education. Tests for the level include looking up telephone numbers in a directory, reading a timetable and following a basic recipe. Adults whose literacy level would not enable them to pass these tests are described as "functionally illiterate" and estimates at the beginning of the 21st century were that one in five citizens of post-school age in the United Kingdom – more than seven million people – could be thus defined. This extent of illiteracy is apparently acceptable, given that the official target for improvement in current school literacy achievement is that 80 per cent of primary school children should pass the tests – leaving one in five pupils functionally illiterate. Great Britain and the United States share the poorest literacy performance figures of any comparable 'developed' nations worldwide.

fuchsia   A common genus of garden plant, and surely the most commonly misspelled of all plant names. Pronounced FEW sha, it commemorates German botanist Leonhard Fuchs (1501–66).

fulfil   Note spelling of the verb. The noun is fulfilment, but it's fulfilled and fulfilling. American English, confusingly, uses both fulfill and fulfil.

further   See farther.

G

Gaelic Pre-English language of the British Isles still in use particularly in the Scottish Highlands and Ireland. It is a matter of regional pride that in Scotland, the word Gaelic is pronounced 'gah-lik' and in Ireland 'gay-lik.' The language is said to survive in these regions because their Celtic populations were not, as they were in England, overrun by the Romans in the last century BC.

gaff and **gaffe** A gaff is a pole tipped with a hook for landing fish. A gaffe is a social blunder. To blow the gaff is to give away a secret.

gay Now standard English for homosexual, gay was first used in this application in the 1930s to identify members of a community whose more intimate practices were then publicly deplored, and illegal. Gay 'came out' as a term for general use in 1969 with the founding in the United States of the Gay Liberation Front. The word is believed (by the Oxford dictionaries) to derive from Old High German *wahi* ('pretty') entering English via French in the 14th century, by then denoting joyful or brightly coloured. These meanings are retained, but the use of gay in any sense other than homosexual is now rare. In 17th-century English, the word became associated with dissipation and by the mid-19th century a woman described as gay would be taken for a prostitute. In the 21st century, gay is expected to diminish in use as the prime identifier of homosexual men ('lesbian' is preferred by many women) and might, ironically, be displaced by the still-pejorative 'queer.' Gay itself, meanwhile, is now in use among young heterosexuals as an alternative to 'sad.'

geezer The slang word similar to 'bloke' derives from the French *guiser*, a mime artist. It is not related to the hot water spring or apparatus, a geyser, even though the two words are pronounced the same way.

gender One of the few concessions to simplicity in English, particularly from the point of view of foreigners learning the language, is the absence of gender for nouns. The definite article 'the' is universal – unlike for example, French with *la* and *le*, or German with *der*, *die* and (neuter) *das*. Similarly, English adjectives do not take masculine/feminine forms, with the few exceptions of words adopted from foreign languages – such as blond(e) from French.

genitive In grammar the possessive case of a noun or pronoun. In the sentence "That's not Sheila's book, it's mine" Sheila's and mine are respectively a genitive noun and a genitive pronoun.

genre Buzz word that originates in the phrase 'genre painting' first used to describe the depiction of scenes from everyday life. The word has long since migrated into the jargon of film and literary criticism and is really just a fancy synonym for 'type' or 'style.'

Georgian In architecture, it refers to a neoclassical style approximately coincident with the reigns of the successive Hanoverian kings George I to George IV (1714–1830). There is another Georgian era, defined by the successive reigns of Windsor kings George V and George VI (1910–1952) but really only remembered for the brief period up to 1920 known for Georgian literature, particularly the poetry of major figures including Robert Graves, A E Housman, Walter de la Mare, John Masefield, Wilfred Owen and Siegfried Sassoon.

geriatric How odd that this word has entered the 21st century as a term of contempt. It has migrated from the branch of medicine dedicated to the care of old people (geriatrics, from Greek *geras* meaning old age and *iatros*, doctor) and has become synonymous with decrepit or confused. Don't use it in this way.

German It is a quirk of the German language that all nouns – not just proper nouns – are written with an initial capital letter. So, for correctness (or just to show off your knowledge) use the capital when lifting words from German, in phrases such as "he relished the *Schadenfreude* of his rival's ill-fortune" or "she was very much more than a humble *Hausfrau*."

German – borrowings from There has been a steady trickle of German words into English use, particularly since the 19th

gerund

century. Familiar examples (so familiar the initial capital can be dispensed with – see previous entry) are angst, blitz, delicatessen, flak, poltergeist, quartz, rucksack, waltz.

gerund A verb participle used as a noun. In the phrase 'the proof of the pudding is in the eating' the word 'eating' is a gerund. From Latin *gerundium*, the gerund of *gerere* (to do). The term gerundive has no application in English, but in Latin it is a verb form ending in *-ndus* and conveying the adjectival meaning 'that needs to be done.'

get This word is now commonly being substituted for 'have,' as in "Can I get a Big Mac?" On no account is this acceptable.

gherkin and **ghetto** Note spellings.

gipsy See gypsy.

girlie The term was once confined to a type of mildly titillating material, as in girlie calendars or girlie magazines. But now the word occurs much more frequently in the 21st-century phrase 'girlie man' for a kind of male deemed lacking in some or all of the masculine virtues, though not necessarily a homosexual. Note spelling girlie, never girly.

glottal stop Symptom of poor diction in which consonant sounds are substituted by the opening or closing of the glottis between the vocal cords in the windpipe. We all know the effect by sound, but it is very difficult to convey it in the written word. The answer is to avoid attempting to do so.

GM Genetically modified, as in crops. But the initials also stand for the world's largest manufacturing company, General Motors, and in the UK for the gallantry award, the George Medal.

gobsmacked a word of ineffable vulgarity that should never be used by writers outside direct reported speech. Irish slang.

God and **god** It remains, thus far, a convention in the English-speaking Christian world that the deity is referred to with an initial capital. Lower case gods are understood to be those of ancient myth or more recent metaphor.

googol A very large number indeed, specifically 10 to the power of 100. It's an invented word and not to be confused with Google, the internet search engine.

Goth A worldwide youth 'counterculture' launched, according to some popular historians, by British pop singer Ziggy Stardust – known for his black clothing and eyeliner, white face and piercings – in 1979. The themes of androgyny and mortality are central. The Goth movement has just about survived into the 21st century, but owes its origins to a rather earlier 'Gothic' revival than that of post-punk Britain in the late 1970s. In literature, the theme was introduced by writer and politician Horace Walpole with his Gothic novel *Castle of Otranto* in 1764. Gothic fiction progressed via landmarks such as Mary Shelley's *Frankenstein* of 1818 and the works of Edgar Allen Poe (d 1846) to the renowned Gothic 'Titus' pastiches of Mervyn Peake (d 1968). 'Gothic horror' novels maintain the tradition into the 21st century – notably from the pen of American author Stephen King. Walpole, who titled *Castle Otranto* 'A Gothic Story' meaning merely to say it was a medieval tale, is also primarily credited with the revival of Gothic architecture in Britain. The wealthy son of Britain's first prime minister, Sir Robert Walpole, he bought a house at Strawberry Hill in Twickenham, Middlesex in 1747 and set about turning it into a 'Gothicized' castle – in the style of the vertical architecture that had held sway from the 12th to the 16th centuries but had been almost-entirely displaced by neo-classical and Italianate design thereafter. The term Gothic seems to have been first used disparagingly by Renaissance architects to dismiss the soaring style of high-arched, buttressed and spired churches of the Middle Ages. The connection with the Goths, a Germanic race who settled on the shores of the Black Sea in the 2nd century AD and whose tribes, the Ostrogoths and Visigoths, displaced the Romans in much of Italy, France and Spain, seems to derive from the belief that savage 'Gothic' had overwhelmed civilised 'Classical' as the dominant culture. Use the capital letter. From Latin *Gothi*, for the original tribe.

gourmand and **gourmet** Simple distinction here: a gourmand eats a lot and a gourmet cares a lot about what he eats.

government

government Where you are referring to a particular government, use an initial capital. "The Government is in disarray after yesterday's announcement" takes the capital because it refers to the current government in office. Likewise, "the French Government refused to back down" employs the capital because the administration in question is specified as the present one. Without the capital, the phrase could be taken to refer to any French government, past or present. When writing about previous governments, avoid the capital, as in "the government of the day failed in its duty."

gram The metric weight measurement can now safely be written in this abbreviated form instead of the former 'gramme.'

grammar Reports of the death of grammar have been exaggerated. Traditionalists complain that grammar, in the sense of a set of formal rules for 'correct' use of the language, is no longer taught in schools and that this contributes to a steepening decline in the clarity of both spoken and written English. But there is no real evidence that grammar is absent from the school curriculum. In its advice to teachers, the official National Curriculum for England states: "In writing, pupils should be taught to use correct spelling and punctuation and follow grammatical conventions." Allegations that 'sloppy' usage is invading the language have been made by successive generations for centuries and are a continuing reassurance that English changes with the times.

-graphy Words with this suffix refer to a description in writing, as in biography, a life story or geography, description of the physical world. Greek *grapho* (to write). More recent photography, radiography etc are descriptive, even though not in the medium of the written word.

Greats Esoteric, not to say exclusive, term for the honours course in classics, philosophy and ancient history (also known in the Latin as *literae humaniores*) at Oxford University.

Greek Much of English vocabulary derives from the language of ancient Greece, but principally via Latin, because the Romans themselves were greatly influenced by the culture of the Greeks and borrowed their words as well as their ideas.

Greek theatre   Today's drama industry – in theatre, cinema and television – owes its origins to ancient Greece and in particular to an Athenian tyrant. Pisistratus (600–527BC), was the first ruler of Athens to confront a civic problem that had been escalating for generations. Every spring, the populace celebrated the rites of Dionysus, a wine-soaked festival in the streets, where crowds gathered to hear priests in *chorus*, declaiming the legend of the man-god born of a union between mortal princess Semele and mighty Zeus himself.

Athenian leaders disdained the debauch, but dared not intervene between the people and their favourite god. Banning the rites might provoke revolution. Pisistratus found an ingenious compromise. He sublimated the rites into a municipal event. Celebrants were given a dedicated enclosure in the heart of the city, at the foot of the Acropolis itself. A circular space (*orchestra*), it had an altar to the wine-god at its centre where the chorus was encouraged to congregate. Before long, to improve spectators' view, wooden benches were arranged in tiers on the lower slopes of the Acropolis, in a semi-circle. The complete, stone-built theatre ultimately had seats for 14,000.

In this Theatre of Dionysus chorus evolved into dialogue and plot. The city commissioned poets to fashion the ancient legends into *drama* ('action' in Greek), with prizes on offer for the best efforts. Thus did the narrative works of Aeschylus and Sophocles, Aristophanes and Euripides underpin the art of playwriting in Greece, and the traditions of drama throughout the western world. Performances continue in the original theatre to this day.

grill and **grille**   A grill is a device for cooking. A grille is an arrangement of metalwork to protect a door, window or other aperture.

grotesque   The original meaning is theatrically distorted or ugly, as in a grotesque caricature. But the word grotty, its more plebeian descendant, merely means dirty or tatty. Italian *grottesca* (grotto-like).

group   A collective word which should be treated as such – in the singular. "The group is on tour", not "the group are on tour."

grow

grow   The transitive verb, as to grow a beard or a crop in the sense of cultivation, has lately been extended in the language of commerce into the phrase 'to grow the business' – synonymous with enlarge.

gypsy   The spellings gipsy and gypsy are both in widespread use, but gypsy is just a little ahead.

Habsburg and **Hapsburg** The correct name for the most powerful and enduring royal dynasty in European history is Habsburg, after the castle of Habichtsburg in the Upper Rhine, built by the family of the first Count of Habsburg in the 11th century. The word Hapsburg is a latter-day invention.

hackneyed Overused and redundant, as in a hackneyed phrase. Writers must beware. See cliché.

hagiography Originally, the life story of a saint, but now a term of contempt for any biography deemed too reverential. Greek *hagios* (holy).

haiku The Japanese verse form, usually in three lines of successively five, seven and five syllables, has been imitated in English, even by respectable poets, since the 19th century. It is now a common exercise form in the teaching of English literature in British schools. Traditionally, the poem expresses a single idea or word picture, as:

> Haiku is to verse
> What a meal of sushi is
> To the staff of life

hail and **hale** As well as the sense of to rain down, as in blows or hailstones, to hail is to greet or signal, as in the idiom 'hail fellow, well met,' or to hail a taxi. Hale is an adjective meaning strong, as in the idiom 'hale and hearty.'

hallo See hello.

Hallowe'en The festival of 31 October is correctly written with an initial capital, and apostrophe. The name is a contraction of 'All Hallows Even' – the eve of All Saints Day.

hangar Aircraft shelter. Not to be confused with clothes hanger.

hello The familiar term of greeting has been recorded in

hence

English only a short time. It is said first to have been written down, in form of 'hullo' in the novel *Tom Brown's School Days* by Thomas Hughes in 1857. The first 'hallo' appears in 1864, and 'hello' not until 1883. Today, the Oxford dictionaries state that hello is the majority sound and spelling and that hallo and hullo are variants of it.

hence   Besides its sense of 'therefore,' the word means 'from this time' and long ago also meant 'from this place.' Hence, there is no need to use the word from in conjunction with hence. "Ten years hence" is correct. "Ten years from hence" is nonsense.

hendiadys   Figure of speech in which a single idea is expressed by two words connected by the conjunction 'and.' Examples are 'nice and easy' and 'doom and gloom.' Greek *hen dia duoin* (one thing by two).

heroine   Note that a female hero takes the 'e.' Heroin is an illicit version of the drug diamorphine.

hetero-   Words with this prefix describe difference. Heterosexual means attracted to the opposite sex. Greek *heteros* (other).

heterogeneous   Now widely used adjective for people, things or ideas diverse in character. Note spelling – there is no such word as 'heterogenous.' Greek *heteros* (other) and *genus* (race).

high-tech   Originally, an architectural style of the 1970s, but now describing any advanced technology. Also written hi-tech.

historian and **historic**   There is a horrible tendency to qualify these words with the indefinite article 'an.' Politicians seem to believe the phrase "an historic moment" conveys more gravity than the correct "a historic moment." The rule is that the very few English words that take 'an' before a sounded 'h' are those that have been lifted directly from French – thus the now old-fashioned 'an hotel.' Before pompously writing "an historic moment" ask yourself, would you write "an history teacher"?

hoard   See horde.

hocus pocus   Once the opening phrase of a conjurer's chant, this term for any kind of trickery or deceit owes its origins to the Latin

Mass – *hoc est corpus meus* (this is my body). The Mass was ridiculed during the Reformation of the 16th century.

homo-   The prefix signifies sameness, not maleness. It's from the ancient Greek word *homoios*, meaning like or same. Homosexual thus describes someone, of either gender, with same-sex inclinations.

homoeopathy This branch of 'alternative' medicine – alternative, that is, to the currently dominant 'allopathic' medicine – takes its name from Greek *homoios* (like) and *patheia* (suffering). It works on the principle of 'treat like with like.' Patients are given very small doses of medicines which, administered in larger measure, would cause or aggravate the ailment in question. Allopathic medicine, taking its name from Greek *allos* (other) operates on the reverse principle – of treatment with drugs which directly oppose the symptoms of the disease. It is a courtesy to its practitioners and subscribers to spell out homoeopathy in full and to eschew the increasingly common 'homeopathy,' an American form.

homogeneous Being of similar type, culture or race. Note spelling. Homogenous is another word altogether, applying only to human biology, and no longer in common use. Greek *homoios* (same) and Latin *genus* (race).

homonym   a word that sounds the same as another; as, bare and bear; berth and birth; cede and seed; cord and chord; gilt and guilt; hoard and horde; rain, reign and rein. Also, a single word with two or more distinct meanings. An example is the verb to shed, meaning to take off, as distinct from the noun shed, a kind of outhouse. Greek *homoios* (same) and *onoma* (name).

homophone   a homonym (see entry) but only a word that sounds identical to another and not one spelt the same. Greek *homoios* (same) and *phone* (sound or voice).

homosexual   It describes a type of behaviour of unquestionably ancient provenance, but the word itself is modern, not appearing in English dictionaries until the early part of the 20th century. Curiously, use of the word was expressly forbidden to officers of

hopefully

London's Metropolitan Police in an edict of 2001. The force's handbook of that year advised that " 'homosexual' is a medical term used to criminalise lesbians, gay men and bisexuals in the 19th century."

hopefully   This adverb has two distinct uses. One is in the sense of 'full of hope' or 'in a hopeful way,' as in "the punter hopefully awaits the outcome of the race." The other is in the sense of 'it is hoped that,' as in "hopefully the punter's horse will win." This second use, in which the adverb qualifies the whole sentence, is deemed bad English by some pedants, because there is a remote possibility the sense could be confused. The example here could be interpreted to mean "the punter's horse will win in a hopeful way." There may be something in this, so do employ the word hopefully – and similarly tricky adverbs such as gladly, happily, regretfully and sadly – with care.

horde and **hoard**   A horde is a great crowd, especially a rabble of soldiery. A hoard is a hidden stock or store, especially of valuables.

horror   Beware the use of this word and its variants, horrible, horrid, horrific, horrifying and horrendous. All have been so overused, first in straight reportage and drama and subsequently in satire, that they have lost much of their power to convey the true unpleasantness they are sometimes intended to express.

hubris   In Greek drama, hubris was the excessive pride that drove mortals to the folly of defying the gods. Hubris was punished by Nemesis, an avenging goddess, who would strip the proud of their wealth or influence. These picturesque words survive intact in 21st-century English and it seems likely they will continue to pertain to the human condition for the foreseeable future.

humorous   Note spelling.

hyper-   The very many words with this prefix tend to express something heightened or excessive, as in hyperactive and hypersensitive. Greek *huper* (above).

hyperbole   Figure of speech for an overstatement of a kind not intended to be taken literally, as "I've seen *The Sound of Music* millions of times." Greek *huper* (above) and *ballo* (to throw).

hyphen   In the present century, we have become accustomed to American presidents who show no evident interest in the scholarly use of English. So it is salutary to recall Woodrow Wilson, the law academic who was president of Princeton long before he became president of the United States in 1916. Wilson was a prescriptive grammarian who wrote, apparently without irony, that "the hyphen is the most un-American thing in the world." He also introduced the policy of Prohibition, in the hope of curing America's perceived addiction to alcohol. In neither of these proscriptions did he remotely succeed.

Use of hyphenation continues to be a source of headaches for writers. Hyphenated nouns are identified as such in dictionaries: get-together, set-up, washing-up. But there is a tendency, especially in American English, to drop the hyphen, creating new words such as setup – though, mercifully, not yet gettogether or washingup. For the moment, use a hyphen in two-word nouns where it has a function. Thus a high-flyer, for someone who actually or metaphorically flies high rather than a flyer who is high for some unassociated reason. Where the modifying is by a verb, as in a flying doctor, a hyphen is not used.

But use of the hyphen to modify sense in a phrase is less straightforward. It is a matter of thinking clearly about what you are trying to say. In the sentence 'The Mousetrap is the world's longest running play' the sense is, strictly, that The Mousetrap is the longest play about running, because the adjective longest appears to modify the participle running rather than the noun play. Put the hyphen in to make longest-running, and the sense becomes clear. It's worth the trouble.

An awkward problem can be that of common modifiers to a single object. 'A group of 16- and 17-year-olds' may look odd, but the use of the hyphen after 16 does have a useful function. Other examples of odd but correct use include "The main television and radio stations are government-owned and -controlled" (*Spectator* 2001). Had the writer (or sub-editor) not appended the second hyphen, the word controlled could be taken to refer to control by a person or body other than the government. But in another instance, the *Spectator* got it wrong with "Union flag-waving" in a

2002 article. The writer meant to describe overtly nationalist activity, but the sense looks much more like flag waving by a trades union. The habit of displaying the Union Jack should be described as 'Union-flag waving', or in a modifying phrase 'a Union-flag-waving mob.'

Do not add hyphens where an adverb modifies an adjective, as in 'she was a fiercely loyal wife' or even in 'he was accompanied by his fiercely loyal wife.' The adverb fiercely obviously qualifies the wife's loyalty, not the wife herself.

-hypo The many words with this prefix tend to express something reduced or below normal, as in hypothermia (loss of body heat) and hypoxia (lack of oxygen). Greek *hupo* (below).

hysteron-proteron One of the dottier figures of speech, this is a device by which the rational order of a phrase is reversed, usually for comic effect, as "bred and born." Greek *husteron proteron* (one in front of the other).

I

I The nominative personal pronoun and, according to language analysts, the most-used word in English speech. 'I' qualifies the verb, not the other way round. 'My husband and I arranged to meet a friend in the park' is correct, but 'a friend agreed to meet my husband and I in the park' is not. Where the first person is described in any case other than the nominative, the pronoun is 'me.' Uniquely in the language, this one-letter word, lacking a 'proper' meaning or association (as in God and His), is always written as a capital. The word is a shortening of Middle English *ich*.

i before e except after c Useful rule of spelling where syllable sounds as 'ee', but there are exceptions: caffeine, codeine, either, Neil, neither, protein, seize, Sheila, weir, weird. Words ending in -feit are an arguable further exception, but only if you are mispronouncing them, as in counterfeit, which is correctly spoken as 'counterfit' not as 'counterfeet.'

iambic Style of poetry-writing in which the lines are formed by iambuses – pairs of syllables, the first short and the second longer. Thus the sound of iambic verse is 'dee-dum, dee-dum, dee-dum.' The dreaded iambic pentameter is a line of five iambuses and thus of ten syllables. Poet John Keats's *Ode to a Nightingale* is an example:

> 'My heart/ aches and/ a drow/sy numb/ness pains
> My sense/ as though/ of hem/lock I/ had drunk'

-ible For words ending in -ible (as distinct from those ending in -able) see -able.

idiom Collectively, the part of any language that is best known to its native speakers, as the idiom of English football managers is filled with expressions specific to the culture – "Over the moon," "Sick as a parrot" and so on. Individually, idioms are phrases whose

idiosyncrasy

meanings are well understood by some and incomprehensible to others, as in "Splice the mainbrace" and "dead cat bounce."

idiosyncrasy   This is a weasel word when pluralized, as in "I like her in spite of her idiosyncrasies." A person has one idiosyncrasy only because the word denotes the whole character, as identified by their manner or the way they think. Greek *idios* (own) *sun* (with) and *krasis* (mixture).

illusion   See allude.

imitative   Dictionaries describe words as imitative when they resemble the sound or action they describe. Crash, plop and whizz are all imitative.

imperative   In grammar, the mood of command. In "Come here!" the verb 'come' is in the imperative.

imperfect tense   In grammar the tense of a verb describing the progress of an action in the past. In "he was laughing" the verb 'was' is the imperfect tense of 'be'.

impinge   In the participle, use impingeing, not impinging.

imply   See infer.

inapt and **inept**   Inapt is now used to mean inappropriate or unsuitable, as in "his inapt remark caused embarrassment." Inept means unskilful, as in "he was far too inept to take on DIY tasks." The two words were once more interchangeable, and have the same root, from Latin in (not) and aptus (apt), but the meanings should now be differentiated.

incredible   Universal term used in speech to mean amazing, extraordinary etc, should not be used in written descriptions. Correctly it means unbelievable, from Latin *in* (not) and *credo* (to believe).

indefinite article   In grammar, a and an (*qv*).

Indian   The languages of the Indian subcontinent, in particular Hindustani, have contributed extensively to the vocabulary of English. British trade with the subcontinent from the 16th century, culminating in colonisation under the East India Company and later the Crown has brought about a continuous migration of new words. Some of those taken directly or via adaptation include: bangle, bungalow, calico, cheroot, chintz, chit, dinghy, gingham, jodhpurs, juggernaut, jungle, loot, pagoda, pashmina, pukka, shampoo, shawl, tea, toddy, veranda.

indirect object   In grammar, it is the secondary object qualified by a verb in a sentence. In "Give me the money" the pronoun 'me' is the indirect object and 'money' the direct object.

infer and **imply**   To infer is to draw a conclusion, as in "I infer from what you say that you consider the defendant guilty." To imply is to suggest or insinuate, as "are you implying the defendant is guilty?"

infinitive   The infinitive form of a verb is the one by which it is recognised, and identified in dictionaries with the preposition 'to', as in to be, to go, to fly etc. It is the form of the verb without the inflexions of case and tense.

inflection   In grammar, the varying forms or endings (also called suffixes) of words according to the gender, person, tense and so on. In English, nouns have three inflections, the plural (house/houses, mouse/mice), the possessive (John/John's) and gender (actor/actress, blond/blonde). Pronouns have inflections according to their case: 'his' is the possessive inflection of 'he.' Verbs are inflected according to tense (come/came) and case (I do/she does). The inflections in adjectives are comparative (tall/taller) and superlative (tallest). From Latin *inflectere* (to change direction). Also spelled inflexion.

-inge   Verbs ending with this (binge, cringe, hinge, impinge, singe, whinge) present problems in the adverbial or participle form. Which is correct: Whingeing or whinging? Bingeing or binging? Singeing or singing? These three examples, according to the dictionaries, take the 'e.' But the same dictionaries plump for cringing, hinging and impinging. I believe this is wrong. Cringing, hinging and impinging simply don't appear like real words – they look more like misspellings or misprints. My own advice is to be consistent. Always include the 'e' – and thus leave no reader in doubt as to what word you're using.

innit   Slang version of 'isn't it' needs careful use (if any) in reported speech. It is now a common synonym for verbal spacers such as 'you know' and 'I mean.'

In(n)uit   The correct form to describe the indigenous peoples of Greenland and Arctic America. The old term 'Eskimo' (meaning an eater of raw flesh) is deemed demeaning in the 21st century.

inquiry   See enquiry.

instil   Note spelling in British English.

intellectual and **intelligent**   An intellectual is someone identified as a thinker who is separated from worldly concerns. An intelligent person is merely someone who can think with reasonable facility.

intensive   In grammar, an adjective or adverb is an intensive when it is used to intensify the meaning of the word it qualifies. In the phrase 'absolutely ghastly' the word 'absolutely' is the intensive.

interment   Burial. Beware confusion with internment (*qv*).

International Phonetic Alphabet   Dictionaries in English and many other languages use this register of letters and symbols to indicate pronunciations. The drawback is that to most of us, the symbols used are incomprehensible, and can only be understood with the aid of the complex key in the dictionary's introductory section.

   In this book, indications of pronunciation are given in a simplified form.

internment   Imprisonment, especially as under the British government's policy in Northern Ireland in the 20th century of detaining political and terrorist suspects. Beware confusion with interment (*qv*).

interpersonal   A word beloved of some sections of government, but to be avoided by all rational writers.

interrogative   Questioning. In grammar, the sentence "What time is it?" is interrogative and the pronoun "who?" is interrogative. Latin *inter* (between) and *rogare* (to ask). There are five interrogative pronouns: what, which, who, whom and whose.

into Always distinguish between the preposition into as in 'he went into the pub' and the preposition-infinitive phrase 'in to' as 'he went in to get a drink.'

intransitive In grammar, use of verbs is either transitive or intransitive. A transitive verb directly qualifies a noun. 'To sell' is transitive, as in "do you sell milk?" An intransitive verb is one that does not directly qualify an object. 'To think' is intransitive, as in "do you think you could sell me some milk?" Countless verbs can be used either transitively or intransitively.

intrusive 'r' In spoken English, this is the deplored tendency to mispronounce words ending in a vowel (usually -a) where they immediately precede another word beginning with a vowel, as in Pamela(r) Anderson. The late actor John Gielgud (1904–2000) had a maxim: "There is no 'r' in vanilla ice."

inverted commas See quotation marks.

irony A word with many interpretations. What is irony? Scholarly opinions, regrettably, differ, but the literary origins are believed to be known. It all begins with the ancient Greek word *eiron*, meaning a dissembler – someone who says one thing, but by his actions clearly shows he means something else. In Greek theatre, the theme was developed into dramatic irony. In *Oedipus Tyrannus*, written around 429BC by Sophocles, the audience enjoys the exquisite irony of knowing the principal character has killed his father and married his mother before Oedipus himself discovers the appalling truth. Irony thus becomes a useful tool for authors, a means of generating the kind of dramatic tension that keeps audiences on the edges of their seats or readers turning the pages.

But irony has much wider significance. It is said to be an ingrained trait of English behaviour. The 'British understatement' – "I don't like wars; they have uncertain outcomes" attributed to Queen Elizabeth I – supposedly employs irony both to show a grasp of, but also a dismissive view of, an unpalatable fact. Irony is identified with sophistication. A well-informed person might use irony in a perverse way both to establish his certain knowledge and to suggest that he wears his worldliness lightly, as in Oscar Wilde's quip that "The trouble with socialism is that it takes up too many evenings."

Irony is a refuge from sincerity. The young lover who wishes to express true adoration of his girlfriend but cannot bear directly to say "I love you" camouflages his declaration with an ironic "I lurv you" in imitation of pop-song style – leaving the object of his affection to wonder what he really means. Such is the nature of love, and of irony.

irregular verb   A verb that conjugates (*qv*) with non-standard inflexions (*qv*). 'To be' is an irregular verb conjugating into several differing inflexions: I am, you are, he/she is, we/they are. There are 283 irregular verbs in English.

-is   Words with this ending commonly take the ending -es in the plural, following the Latin form. Thus the plural of crisis is crises, and not crisises.

-ise and **-ize**   The verb ending -ize might seem American, but in fact has been dominant in British English for 500 years. Only a few common verbs invariably take the -ise ending, including all those ending -cise, -prise (exception is to prize, as in to value) and -vise plus advertise, chastise, despise, disguise, franchise, merchandise and surmise.

italics   In typography, the script version of a typeface.

its   The possessive neuter pronoun, as in "the car was stripped of its wheels." Note no apostrophe is used in any circumstances, because the word is specifically possessive.

it's   Abbreviation of it is. Beware confusion with 'its' immediately above.

J

jackknife Note that this verb, meaning to double up like a jack knife (American term for English penknife) is spelled as one word with two ks.

Jacobean In English history, it identifies the reign of James I from 1603 to 1625 and in particular the architecture of the period, which differed from the 'Elizabethan' style of the preceding monarch.

Jacobite In English history, it identifies supporters of King James II who stayed loyal after his abdication in 1688.

jasmine As in the shrub and the tea, spell always with the 'e.' From Persian *yasamin*.

jejune It means barren (as in land) but of late has extended deep into metaphor, now being a smart way of saying dull, unsophisticated or shallow. A word that looks well set for a prosperous 21st century, as in this sneering review from *The Times* on the new *Grove Dictionary of Music and Musicians* published in 2001: "Many entries on popular performers … read as if they are aimed at readers of *Smash Hits*, so jejune is their musical analysis." Latin *jejunus* (starving).

Jew It describes a person of Hebrew descent or of the Judaic religion. Because the term Jew has at some times acquired offensive nuance, it is frequently substituted with 'Jewish person.' This might be political correctness. Or it might simply be good manners.

jihad Now in everyday use this Arabic word is identified by the Oxford dictionaries as meaning "holy war undertaken by Muslims against unbelievers." The alternative spelling 'jehad' has not survived into the 21st century.

just deserts Beware the common misspelling 'desserts.' Deserts are what you deserve; desserts are what some restaurants call their puddings.

Kant See Cant.

ken To know, now largely confined to Scottish vernacular, but once common in English. Ken also means knowledge or understanding in the phrase 'beyond our ken' for something incomprehensible.

kenning A figure of speech not widely known before its appearance among the terms laid down for inclusion in "pupils' developing vocabulary" as determined by the UK National Literacy Strategy for primary schools in 1998. Kenning turns out to mean a metaphoric representation of a poetically symbolic kind. Thus, according to the Strategy, is 'death bringer' a kenning for sword. From now-rare ken, to know, derived from Old Norse *kenna*.

kidult New word for adults perceived to be in the market for products or services – such as computer games – usually targeted at children.

kitchen-sink drama A lit-crit term that has just about survived into the 21st century. It originally described theatre and early television productions centred on mundane everyday life from the 1950s. Judging by current themes in the same media, neither drama nor life itself has moved on very much.

kitsch Sentimental or tasteless style, particularly in furnishings and art, as "kitsch representations of Princess Diana." A buzzword, from German, that has migrated intact from the early 20th century into the 21st.

knick-knack Use all the ks.

kosher Pronounced 'кон sher', it describes food and food production, and retailing premises, deemed suitable under Jewish law. But it has come also to mean genuine or legitimate in a much wider sense. From Hebrew *kasher* (proper).

L

labyrinthine   This is the usual adjective from labyrinth, meaning a maze of passages and thus anything perplexingly complicated. Labyrinthian is also used, but is less felicitous. Greek *laburinthos*, the maze on Crete in which the Minotaur lived.

ladette   Recent feminisation of 'lad' is still current.

lager lout   Now hackneyed. Avoid.

lama and **llama**   A lama is Buddhist monk. A llama is commonly domesticated South American animal kept for its wool or as a beast of burden.

lamp post   Write as two words.

large   New verb, as in 'larging it' to denote conspicuous displaying of wealth or status. "Dealers larging it in beamers" roughly translates as "Drug traffickers flaunting their ill-gotten gains by driving BMW cars."

lasso   Note spelling in spite of pronunciation 'la soo.' Spanish American from Spanish *lazo*, after Latin *laqueus* (noose).

Latin   The language of the ancient Romans and the principal source of the grammar and vocabulary of English and several other 'Romanic' languages including Italian, French and Spanish.

lay and **lie**   The verb 'to lay' has two distinct uses. One is as the past tense of 'lie' as in, "she lay down to sleep" or "she laid the money on the counter." The other is as a verb in its own right, as in "will you lay the table for six, please?" or "don't you lay a hand on me." It is a reasonable rule to use the verb 'lie' in all other senses.

leak and **leek**   A leak is an unintended escape of water, or information. A leek is a root vegetable.

legend   A legend is an old myth or story passed down several generations by retelling rather than via the written word, and is by definition unverifiable. Legends are not necessarily false. Now

less and **fewer**

that a legend can be a real person, even of our own time, such as "rock legend Freddie Mercury," the context of mythology has lost some of its force in the word. Latin *legere* (to read).

less and **fewer**   See fewer.

lexicon   A dictionary.

Liberal   In British politics, an extinct definition. The Liberal Party, long ago descended from the Whig party, has become the Liberal Democrat Party. No politician can now be identified as a Liberal.

libel   You libel someone if you publish a malicious untruth about them. Besides the very occasional criminal libel, cases are tried under civil law, commonly in front of a jury. The law is complex, but it is a reasonably simple matter to avoid committing libel – by never publishing an untruth, and never publishing anything with malicious intent. Latin *liber* (book).

libretto   The words written for a musical work, usually opera.

lie   See lay.

lifestyle   Ubiquitous noun and adjective corresponds to 'the way we live.' It has been in wide use since the 1980s, originally as marketing jargon connected to the study of consumers' shopping habits. 'Lifestyle marketing' is the targeting of products and services at identified consumer groups.

lig   Recent slang verb meaning to gatecrash or freeload.

lightening   The present participle of the verb to lighten, as in 'the lightening sky at dawn.' Beware confusion with 'lightning' as in 'thunder and lightning.'

like   Only a short time ago the use of the word 'like' in place of 'as if' – as in 'he looks like he's going to have a fit' – was considered a heretical solecism (*qv*). But this usage is now so commonplace that only the most cloistered pedant will raise more than an eyebrow on hearing it. The word is also widely used in place of 'such as' – as in "celebrities such as Tom Cruise." The problem here is that if this statement is made as "actors like Tom Cruise" it appears to imply the existence of actors similar to Tom – who no doubt prides himself on his high degree of individuality and would object to such a remark made about him. So, avoid the lazy use of 'like' in place of 'such as' and confusion such as this will not arise.

likeable   Spell it this way, not as 'likable.'

limerick   The verse form gets its name from the town and county of Limerick in Ireland where it was once the custom for people to gather and improvise poetry. The traditional form is five lines rhyming on the basis of a-a-b-b-a. But diversions from this convention are equally welcome, as:

> There was a young man from Japan
> Who wrote verses that just wouldn't scan.
> The reason for this
> Was he couldn't resist
> Trying to cram far too many words into the last line.

linage and **lineage**   Linage – pronounced 'LY nij' – is a system of payment to writers based on the number of words published. Lineage – 'LIN ee ij' – is the linear descent, or pedigree, of an individual or family.

lingerie   The French word for linen drapery, adopted into English to describe female under-attire, is pronounced natively as 'LANJ er ee.'

lingua franca   It does not mean French, but is the Italian phrase for a Frankish (German) language once used by Italian traders in the Levant. Now, lingua franca is used to mean any language spoken in multi-racial expatriate communities, or the jargon of any other kind of group.

linguistics   The scientific study of language. It encompasses the origins, development and use of all world languages, and the part they have played in human history and civilisation.

lite   Originally coined in the US as a branding term for slimming products such as 'lite spread' and 'lite beer,' this variation on 'light' has now entered the wider language as an increasingly frequent suffix. It is largely derisive, as in the simplified "history lite" presented by celebrity academics on television.

literacy   The ability to read and write.

literal   A literal translation is one in which the original words are converted without interpretation. So, the familiar French phrase *ça va* has a literal translation of 'that goes' but in fact is synonymous with 'OK.' Similarly, a literal sense of words may differ from an allegorical or metaphoric one. Homer's immortal phrase "the wine-dark sea" makes no literal sense, but forms an evocative metaphoric statement.

There is common confusion between 'literal' and 'virtual' but need not be. To say someone is a literal millionaire is to say that is exactly what the person is. To say someone is a virtual millionaire means the person in question is close to being so but is not, in fact, a millionaire. In this sense, literal means much the same as actual.

In editing and proofreading, a literal is a mistake made by the author – such as a misspelling – as distinct from a typographical or keyboard error (typo).

literate   Being able to read and write.

litotes   A fancy word for understatement. Its use in English literature is as old as the language itself, but today it most commonly defines the negative use of a word's opposite in order to give a kind of understated emphasis – as when describing something as 'not bad' when what is meant is good or even very good. In short, a very English instrument of expression. Greek for 'simplicity.'

llama   See lama.

Lord's Prayer   Arguably the best-known tract – religious or otherwise – in the English language, and a prayer once familiar to whole generations in the English-speaking world. The words are those used by Jesus Christ to his disciples as quoted in the New Testament (St Matthew Chapter Six, verses nine to 13) of the Bible. In the edition of the Bible known as the Authorised Version (first published in 1611 under the aegis of King James I) the prayer is written: 'Our Father which art in heaven, Hallowed be thy name. Thy kingdom come. Thy will be done in earth, as it is in heaven. Give us this day our daily bread. And forgive us our debts, as we forgive our debtors. And lead us not into temptation, but deliver us from evil: For thine is the kingdom, and the power, and the glory, for ever. Amen.' The most common version of the prayer today differs mostly in the latter phrases: 'Forgive us our trespasses, as we forgive those who trespass against us. And lead us not into temptation, but deliver us from evil, for thine is the kingdom, the power and the glory, for ever and ever. Amen.' The prayer is included in the *Book of Common Prayer*.

lower case   'Small' letters – as distinct from capital letters – are known to printers and publishers as lower case, as distinct from upper case, or capital, letters.

lyric   The words to a popular song, but also the style of meditative poetry written as odes, sonnets etc, as 'the lyric verse of John Keats.' Greek *lurikos* (lyre).

M

ma'am   This contraction of 'madam' is the correct form of address when speaking to the Queen. 'Your Majesty' is used only in formal circumstances.

madam and **madame**   When addressing a letter to an unidentified woman, the spelling is madam. The French madame is used only for the married women of that nation, usually abbreviated, as in Mme Chirac. In less formal use, as in "she's a right little madam," use the English spelling. The one exception is the female 'madame' of a brothel – a legacy of the long-extinct notion that all such women were French.

magnum opus   A great work, usually identified as the major masterpiece of a given writer or artist, as *War and Peace* is the magnum opus of Leo Tolstoy. Latin, but now an everyday term that need not be keyed in italics.

makeover   When denoting a new look, write as one word. As a verb, as "he wants me to make over a large sum of money to him" write as two words.

malapropism   The tendency to muddle the use of words dates back long before the first appearance of Mrs Malaprop in Richard Sheridan's delirious comedy *The Rivals* in 1775, but the pretentious old snob's name has been inseparably attached to this form of solecism (qv) ever since. Among her memorable lines from the play is this description of her romantic niece Lydia Languish: "She's as headstrong as an allegory on the banks of the Nile."

manifest and **manifold**   The adjective manifest means obvious, as in "his wealth is manifest." The adjective manifold means many and varied, as in "her virtues are manifold."

mantra   Buzz word for an oft-repeated, familiar or hackneyed phrase often associated with a given group, or cause. Originally, a repetitive sound or word used in Buddhist and Hindu meditative chant as an aid to concentration.

marrowsky   The same as spoonerism (*qv*), and also as a verb, to utter a spoonerism. Said to derive from Polish Count Marrowski, who suffered the same habit of garbling his words as our own Dr Spooner.

marshal   Note one 'l' only. Marshall is American. The word derives from Old French *mareschal*. Beware confusion with martial, an adjective originally meaning of Mars (either as the planet or the mythical god of war) and now used for warlike or, as in martial law, arbitrary.

may or **might**   Although now used as if entirely interchangeable, these two verbs do have distinct meanings. "You may go to the ball" means Cinderella has permission to go. "You might go to the ball" means Cinderella has the possibility, but not the certainty, of going.

medi(a)eval   The middle 'a' is now disappearing from the spelling of this adjective, denoting the period of history known as the Middle Ages. Latin *medius* (middle) and *aevum* (age). See Middle Ages.

media and **medium**   Media is the plural form of medium. In communications, broadcasting is a medium and newspaper publishing is another medium. Combined, they are the media. It is correct, therefore, to say and to write "the media are … " Latin *medium* (middle).

meiosis   Figure of speech expressing an understatement, as a multiple motorway pile-up described as "a bit of a prang." Greek *meion* (less).

melodrama   Contemptuous term for a play or film with unconvincingly over-dramatised plot and performances. Now commonly applied to behaviour, as in "Don't be so melodramatic." Greek *melos* (music) and *drao* (to act).

meta-   Words beginning with the common suffix usually denote some kind of change, as in the metabolism that changes food into energy and metamorphosis, the process by which insects change from egg to larva to pupa to adult. Greek *meta* (after).

metaphor

metaphor   Figure of speech in which information or ideas are conveyed by imaginative association. Metaphors occur in the oldest of writings, such as the "wine-dark sea" and "rosy-fingered dawn" in the *Iliad* and *Odyssey*, believed written by Greek poet Homer in the 8th century BC. Mastering the use of metaphor is a key to successful writing, and always will be.

metaphysical   The roots of metaphysics lie in the deliberations made on the nature of existence by Greek philosopher Aristotle in the 4th century BC. In the 21st century, this branch of philosophy is by no means so narrowly defined, as the term 'metaphysical' is used variously to mean merely theoretical, abstract or other-worldly. The best advice must be to avoid the word unless addressing an audience of philosophers – in which case, use with care.

meter and **metre**   A meter is a device for recording the use of fuel or expiry of time, as in gas meter and parking meter. A metre is a decimal unit of measure, also as in millimetre, kilometre etc.

metonym   A word used with a new or additional sense, as a 'summit' now describes a meeting between heads of state as well as the top of a mountain or as in the transferral of the meaning of 'a domestic' from a household servant to a violent dispute between family members. Greek *metonymia* (changing in name).

metre   See meter.

metrosexual   Buzz word new to the *Oxford English Dictionary* in 2005, metrosexual was coined by journalist Mark Simpson in an article for *The Independent* on 15 November, 1994. He intended the neologism to mean an urban, upper-middle-class person of either sex or sexual preference who takes very great care over their appearance in order to attract sexual partners. But a decade on, the word had altered through usage to mean an urban heterosexual male of any social class who takes personal grooming as seriously as women or homosexual men are sometimes perceived to do – in other words to an unusually fastidious degree. The English football player David Beckham has been widely cited as a metrosexual. The prefix metro-, curiously enough, comes from Greek *meter/metros* (mother) as in *metropolis* (mother city).

mettle   Meaning spirit or courage, as in "the crisis put the government on its mettle" the word should not be confused with its former spelling, metal – now used to describe a family of mineral products (after Greek *metallon*, a mine).

Middle Ages   In Europe as a whole, the thousand years between the collapse of the Roman Empire in the fifth century AD and the capture of Constantinople, capital of the Holy Roman Empire, by Turks in 1453. In Britain, the Middle Ages are the period between our 'Dark Ages' – from the withdrawal of the Roman legions to the first Christian sovereignty of Alfred the Great in the ninth century – and the conclusion of the Wars of the Roses with the accession of the Tudors in 1485. The later Renaissance and early Reformation of the church also coincide broadly with the end of the Middle Ages. Note the adjective for Middle Ages is not Middle Aged, but medieval, from Latin *medius* (middle) and *aevum* (age).

Middle English   The English of Geoffrey Chaucer (1345–1400) is the first form of the language to be readily recognisable to ordinary readers today. Philologists – students of the development of language – say that the period of Middle English dates from about 1100, when the influence of the French-speaking Norman ruling class began to materialise. The Middle English period ends about 1500, coincident with the influence of the Renaissance and subsequent English Reformation.

ming and **mong**   New slang verbs, they are respectively used in the form 'minger' for a person notably lacking in attractiveness, and as the participle 'monged' as in, "he was monged out on amphetamines."

Misspellings: The Top 100   The author's own exhaustive research has arrived at the following 100 most misspelled common words in the language. Some also have their own headings elsewhere.

accommodate	asthma	catarrh	consensus
address	bachelor	cemetery	damn
advertisement	battalion	cereal	definitely
all right	broccoli	cheque	dependent
anoint	campaign	complement	desiccated

desperate	liar	privilege	spaghetti
diarrhoea	licence	proprietor	specific
dinghy	memento	psychiatrist	stationary
disappear	mete	pursue	succour
ecstasy	minuscule	pyjamas	supersede
embarrass	misspelling	quay	surfeit
facetious	mortgage	questionnaire	suspicion
fatigue	necessary	receipt	synonym
forfeit	nous	recommend	their
fulfil	occurred	rehearsal	threshold
graffiti	opinion	rein	thyme
harass	palate	rhyme	tomorrow
heinous	parallel	rhythm	trek
impugn	phenomenon	righteous	waive
inadvertent	physics	sacrilegious	weird
instalment	plumber	sandwich	whether
irresistible	pneumonia	scissors	whose
knowledge	porridge	seize	withhold
lewd	practise	separate	yacht
liaison	precede	skilful	

mixed metaphor The deliberate or accidental mangling of intended metaphors can be one of the foremost joys of the language. A small sampling from my own favourites includes "bite the bullet while it's hot," expressed on more than one occasion by my wife, Sheila, and another of hers, this time rather more cryptic: "there's ointment in everybody's paradise." I am also indebted to the writer Mario Reading for "push the boat out at both ends" and "clutching at the last straws."

mnemonic A device to aid the memory, usually in the form of a phrase or rhyme. Examples are the spelling mnemonic " 'i' before 'e' except after 'c' " and the days-of-the-month jingle, "Thirty days hath September, April, June and November. All the rest have 31, excepting February alone, which has 28 days and 29 in a Leap Year." Greek *mnemon* (mindful). Mnemonic and its variants have the distinction of being the only words in the everyday language beginning with the consecutive letters 'mn.'

modal verb   A kind of auxiliary verb (*qv*) used in a verb group to express intention or possibility. 'Can,' 'must' and 'would' are modal verbs, as in "I can go if I wish to." See also semi-modal verbs.

modern   In chronological terms, modern English describes the language as it has evolved from about 1500, in succession to Middle English. Likewise modern English history, succeeding English medieval history.

modernism   In government policy and thought, modernism is taken to mean a kind of approach to formulating legislation on a current, rather than a historical basis. The actions of a "modernizing" government such as the Labour administration first elected in the UK in 1997 are exemplified by the exclusion of hereditary peers from the law-making process, hunting with dogs, and establishing a compulsory minimum wage to be paid by all employers.

modify   In the language of grammar, modifying is the action or effect of an adjective on a noun and of an adverb on a verb. In the phrase 'a big hole' the adjective 'big' modifies the sense of the otherwise-immeasurable hole. Likewise, in 'she spoke sharply' the adverb 'sharply' modifies the description of her speech.

mono-   Words with this prefix always describe something connected with singularity, from the Greek word *monos* (alone). Thus monogamy means having one spouse, monopoly means something in the ownership of one person or company, and monotony is the boredom arising from exposure to just one theme.

monody   In poetry, a piece of work written in lament for someone who has died. In ancient Greece, it was originally an ode sung by a single actor in a tragic play. Greek *monodos* (singing alone).

monologue   In drama, a long speech by a single actor. It has also come to mean any irritatingly lengthy speech either to an audience or in the midst of conversation. Greek *monologos* (speaking alone).

mood   In grammar, the way a verb is used can always be identified with a 'mood.' There are five distinct ones:

1. Indicative mood expressing a fact: 'He is going'
2. Optative mood expressing a wish: 'Let's go'
3. Imperative mood expressing a command: 'Go!'
4. Interrogative mood expressing a question: 'Is he going?'
5. Subjunctive mood expressing a condition: 'Were he to go ... '

moot   A moot was originally a meeting, or a meeting place such as a courtroom, in the Middle Ages. From Old English *metan* (to meet). The word has evolved into a verb meaning to discuss and an adjective meaning debatable, as in 'a moot point.' Beware confusion with mute, meaning silent.

moral   A story becomes a moral tale or fable when it is effectively a lesson in experience or behaviour. From Latin *mos*, meaning a custom – as in a normally accepted rule of behaviour.

morality play   Drama in which the main characters represent particular qualities of behaviour such as innocence or vengefulness, generosity or greed. This genre seems to have arisen with the 'moralities' of the 1400s in which characters were named with various vices and virtues. The first such recorded play is *Everyman*, translated from Dutch, in which the cast includes Fellowship, Beauty, Knowledge, Good Deeds and so on. The central character, Everyman (identified with no particular vice or virtue), finds in the course of the play that only one of these abstract personifications is ever of any actual use to him in his journey through life – namely Good Deeds. In the centuries since, countless morality plays have been written, but perhaps none that has made the point about the worthlessness of good intentions any better than *Everyman* did more than 500 years ago. Nevertheless, the morality formula continues to be taken up by writers today, and can be expected to proliferate in fiction and particularly in television drama for the foreseeable future.

morph   New verb meaning to change form or shape, as in "she has effortlessly morphed from supermodel to Hollywood star." It derives from the term 'morphing,' describing a digital process of altering images on film. Greek *morphe* (form).

morphology   In linguistics and philology, the study of the form of words, in which they are deconstructed into constituent parts known in the jargon as morphemes.

mortise   The recess that receives the tenon in a lock. Not 'mortice.' From French *mortoise*.

moshing   Recent word descriptive of the jumping, violent head-waving actions of fans at rock-music performances. The term is also applied metaphorically to other inane and solitary practices. Origin is uncertain but may refer to the mushing of the brain feared to be caused by continuous convulsive movement – not to mention the deleterious effects on the senses of amplified music.

Moslem   Now generally written as Muslim. Use the capital letter.

Mr, Mrs   The points formerly used after these contracted titles are just about extinct.

Ms   This relatively recent title, first devised in the United States for business correspondence in the 1950s, has successfully entered the 21st century. But it remains an equivocal form of address, often used in an ironic way to express the enduring belief that women who insist on it are not quite keeping up with the post-feminist Zeitgeist (*qv*).

muppet   Recent term of contempt for a person of low intelligence.

murder your darlings   A catchphrase in the writing industry. It was a piece of advice given regularly to his students by Cambridge Professor of English Sir Arthur Quiller-Couch (1863–1944). His warning was that the passages of their essays students considered the best would very likely turn out to be the sections least liked by their tutors, who wished only to see lucid evidence of comprehension, and not flights of literary creativity. Thus, said Quiller-Couch, students should read through written work before handing it in, and delete their "darlings." Editors in newspapers, magazines and book publishing today continue to be grateful to the professor for this motto, but readers of newspapers and magazines may nevertheless be aware that darlings continue to appear in ill-restrained plenty.

Murphy's law Also known as sod's law, it is the enduring maxim that anything that can go wrong will, eventually, do just that – usually at the most inconvenient moment.

Muslim A member of the Islamic faith. Always use initial capital. The word is Arabic, a participle of the verb *aslama* (to submit) from which the word Islam (submission) is also derived.

MVVD 'Male Vertical Volume Drinker' is supposedly a stereo-typical pub regular.

N

naff   Dr Samuel Johnson's dictionary of 1755 declared a naff to be a kind of tufted sea-bird, but dictionaries now dismiss it as a 20th-century slang adjective for something tasteless or without value. When the Princess Royal, then merely Princess Anne, publicly used the phrase "naff off" in 1980, she spawned a whole naff culture, culminating in the publication of *The Complete Naff Guide*, written by an unlikely team of academics and upper-class twits. They declared all manner of persons and practices to be naff, and the book – little more than a reworking of Nancy Mitford's notorious guide to 'U and non-U' – sold in huge numbers. But it was not without its merits, nominating with profound existentialist insight 10.50 am and 2.45 pm as 'naff times of the day' and giving first place in a listing of 'naff words' to the word naff.

But naff is a charming word deserving adoption in many causes. The writers of the hugely – and enduringly – popular 1970s television series *Porridge*, for example, used the word as a broadcast-friendly substitute for the 'f-word.' When the prison inmates who were the central characters of the comedy said "naff off" or "naffing screws" no one was left in any doubt of the force of their opinions – and yet no offence could be taken by the audience. This is an example of talented use of the language, designed to engage the greatest possible proportion of the audience.

Don't be afraid to use the word naff in the 21st century.

naïf   The French word meaning unaffectedly simple or artless has been fully adopted into English, but the original masculine form has now been displaced by the feminine naïve, probably because it is easier to pronounce clearly. It is now common to write the word as naive without the diaeresis although arguably this might mislead some readers into believing the pronunciation is 'nave' rather than the correct 'ny EEV.' See also naïvety.

naïvety An English word adapted from French *naïveté*, it is becoming more commonly spelled without the diaeresis (¨) of the French original, but – in the era of the computer keyboard – unnecessarily so.

nano- A prefix bound to proliferate in the 21st century as 'nanotechnology' spreads into every sphere of life. It's the science of manipulating materials at the smallest level of their composition, molecules and atoms. Greek *nanos* (dwarf).

nanosecond New word for 'jiffy' or 'blink of an eye' as in, "he was on his feet in a nanosecond." But a nanosecond is a real measure of time, at one billionth of a second.

narcotic The type of drug that induces sleep or insensibility. Don't use 'narcotics' to encompass all kinds of illegal drugs, because not all illegal drugs are narcotics, and many legitimate drugs are narcotics. Greek *narkoo* (to make numb).

narrative The story element in a literary work.

naturalism In literature and art, naturalism is the tendency to represent nature as faithfully as possible. Beware confusion with naturism, the tendency to go about naked.

Neanderthal A fun word with which to dismiss an object, idea or person as hopelessly primitive, old-fashioned or reactionary. Strictly speaking, it refers to an early Stone Age species of man as identified from remains found in 1870 in the Neanderthal, a valley in Germany. The word is now written with or without an initial capital letter.

need to know The phrase migrated from US military jargon into the general language in the late 20th century. It refers to privileged information, as "you will be informed on a need-to-know basis."

nemesis See hubris

neo- This prefix usually denotes a word dealing with the new or the revived, as neophyte, a novice, or neoclassicism, a revival of the style of ancient Greece and Rome. Greek *neos* (new).

neocon Short for neo-conservative, this term is strongly associated with the more right-wing elements of the administrations of US

President George Bush Jnr. But the word neocon was already being used in the 1970s to define some aspects of the American right.

neologism A new word or phrase. Also, a new meaning for an existing word or phrase. Neologism has been a feature of the English language from its birth – thus the unparalleled scale of our vocabulary at more than 600,000 identified words. Neologism also describes the habit of adding new words to the language, as practised by neologists such as William Shakespeare, John Milton and Alexander Pope.

New Age How long the New Age movement, born in 1960s California, can sustain its newness remains to be seen, but the term is certainly very much with us. It describes a culture that proposes alternatives to established modes of government, religious teaching, medical practice and management of the environment, among other things. It is closely identified with protest, particularly against elements of capitalism, commercial farming, nuclear energy and so on.

neither Is there one correct pronunciation? There is not. Neither 'NY ther' nor 'NEE ther' is more correct than the other. The word first appears in English as *nowther* in the Middle Ages.

nerve-racking Avoid nerve-wracking.

neuter In grammar, a word that is neither masculine nor feminine.

nexus Buzz word meaning a connection or interchange; as "the nexus between oil politics and the dollar" (*Spectator*, 2002). Latin *nectere* (to bind).

NGO Non-government(al) organisation is a term lately coined by charities to distinguish themselves from officialdom. Major charities now increasingly work alongside government agencies, armed forces and the United Nations, particularly in the aftermath of natural disasters or conflicts, and need to identify their political neutrality.

nice Overused, yes, but as a word to denote approval as distinct from disapproval without any further qualification, nice certainly has the merit of convenient vagueness. One of the most worthwhile uses of the word is in its sense of precision, as in 'a nice distinction.' The word migrated into medieval English from Old French, complete with its meaning of silly or wanton. It had come into French from the Latin *nescius* (ignorant).

nigger   Taboo word nevertheless in widespread use within black communities.

9/11   Short form for the date 11 September 2001 when New York and Washington were struck in terrorist attacks by hijacked aircraft. This is the American form of the date, in which the month is placed before the day.

no-brainer   Recent noun denotes a task that requires no intellectual input. The sense of the term, which first came into use in the US in the 1970s, is showing signs of extending to books, films and music of such little merit they are described as no-brainers.

nominative   In grammar the case of a noun or pronoun as the subject of the verb in a sentence. In the sentence "he hit me" 'he' is in the nominative case and me is in the accusative case.

none   The word has several meanings and applications, one of which is a contraction of 'not any one of.' In this respect it is a singular pronoun and correctly takes a singular verb. A nice demonstration occurs in an account of spectators at an eruption of Mount Etna reported in *The Times* by Science Editor Nigel Hawkes: "many were thrilled, none was killed." But the pronoun has plural uses too, as in "none but the brave deserve the fair." The word is not a modern contraction of 'not one' as is widely believed, but derives from Old English *nan*, itself a medieval contraction of *ne* (not) and *an* (one).

non-standard English   Term used by educationists to describe bad English. According to the UK Department of Education the five most common "non-standard usages" in England are: subject-verb agreement (they was); formation of past tense (have fell, I done); formation of negatives (ain't); formation of adverbs (come quick); use of demonstrative pronouns (them books).

noon   Midday. Avoid writing 12 noon, an obvious redundancy.

no one   Write as two words, without a hyphen.

normalcy   An oddity from American English, this should be avoided in British English. Use normality.

North East and **North West**   See compass points.

noun   A word or phrase identifying any thing, animate or inanimate, or idea. Latin *nomen* (name).

nouns as verbs   The conversion of nouns into verbs – as in 'please action this recommendation' and 'the art of parenting' – may seem a recent (and to some ears hideous) phenomenon, but it is by no means new.

novel   Described by Dr Samuel Johnson in his *Dictionary* of 1755 as "a small tale, generally of love," the novel has grown up in the intervening years into the senior of the literary forms. Now describes any narrative work of fiction.

numbers   Should they be written as figures or spelled out? In newspaper style, the common ruling is that one to nine are spelled out and all numbers from 10 to 999,999 upwards are set in figures. Round numbers such as one million (or billion) to nine million are spelled out but thereafter incorporate both figures and words, as 10 million or 99 billion. Decimal figures such as 0.6 per cent or 3.7 million use figures whether of a value lower than ten, or not. Avoid beginning sentences with numbers where possible, but where unavoidable, spell the number out, as in "Thirty years ago … "

  Numbers are at the source of numerous words in the language, including bisect (two), decathlon (10), decimate (10), dilemma (two), duplicate (two), hectare (100), millennium (1000), monotonous (one), octopus (eight), pentagon (six), punch (five), quadrangle (four), quarantine (40), quire (four), semester (six), sextant (six), sitar (three), tertiary (three), trivial (three), unitary (one).

O

-o Words ending in 'o' present problems in the plural. Kilo is pluralized kilos, memento can be pluralized as either mementoes or mementos, and tomato is pluralized only as tomatoes. It is impossible to define universal rules for this except that words from other European languages, especially Italian, tend to take the -os ending. The following are the correct forms for most of the commonest words:

Words taking -oes only:

Buffaloes
cargoes
dingoes
dominoes
echoes
embargoes
farragoes
haloes
heroes
mosquitoes
mottoes
negroes
noes
potatoes
tomatoes
torpedoes
vetoes
volcanoes

Words taking either -oes or -os:

banjoes/banjos
fandangoes/fandangos
fiascoes/fiascos
flamingoes/flamingos
grottoes/grottos
innuendoes/innuendos
lassoes/lassos
mangoes/mangos
mementoes/mementos
no-noes/no-nos
porticoes/porticos
salvoes/salvos
stilettoes/stilettos

Words taking -os only:

Anglos
beanos
bimbos
bordellos
calypsos
cellos
chinos
crescendos
demos
discos
egos
folios
ghettos
hairdos
hellos
homos
hypos
impresarios
jumbos
kangaroos
kilos
manifestos
memos
mulattos
patios
photos
pianos
placebos
quangos
radios
scenarios
silos

solos	tangos	twos	yo-yos
sopranos	torsos	videos	zeros
studios	trios	weirdos	zoos

OBE The initials denote an Officer of the Order of the British Empire, just as an MBE denotes a Member of the Order, and CBE a Commander of the Order.

object In grammar, the word or phrase in a sentence that is governed by the verb or by a preposition. In "he bought a book," 'book' is the object; in "she went to school," 'school' is the object.

objective See subjective.

occur Takes a double 'r' in occurred, occurrence, occurring.

OCD Obsessive Compulsive Disorder. A 21st-century diagnosis of a common syndrome now described as a genetic neurological illness rather than the mere psychological complaint of old. Patients are nevertheless still mainly treated with cognitive therapies.

ode Originally a poem set to music, but later any lyrical verse addressed to an object or person, as Keats's *Ode to Fanny* and *Ode on a Grecian Urn*.

oeuvre The work, usually in a collective sense, of a writer, painter or composer. Now often used derisively for the sum of an indifferent artist's achievements, as in, "his oeuvre seems unlikely to outlive him." French.

oik A person, usually male, of an inferior social class or of an uncultured character. Educated middle-class speakers attempting to adopt working-class credentials must beware this word, as its use may betray their true origins. No authentic member of the proletariat employs 'oik.' Dictionaries decline to speculate on the origin of the word beyond asserting that it is a 20th-century device, but possible roots include a corruption from ancient Greek 'hoi' as in 'hoi polloi' (a residual disdainful term for the common populace).

OK In English writing the initial form is more usual than the American 'okay.' In use as a verb, now common, 'okayed' and 'okaying' do, however, seem less awkward than 'OK'd' and 'OK'ing.' The term is originally American and said to stand for Old Kinderhook, the New York birthplace of Martin van Buren (1782–1862), the eighth President of the United States. He adopted the slogan the 'OK candidate' in his senatorial election campaign, and also attributed the meaning 'orl korrect' (a jocular Anglo-Dutch rendering) to the initials to advertise his probity.

Old English   The English language before about 1100. Until that time, the language was largely rooted in the Germanic, Norse and Romanic tongues of successive immigrants into the British Isles. With the coming of the Normans, the era of Old English is gradually succeeded by Middle English (*qv*).

Old Norse   The ancient language of Norway and its outposts until the 14th century, Old Norse is the source from which modern Scandinavian languages largely derive. Many modern English words are derived from Old Norse.

one   Beware the use of 'one' in place of 'I.' "One sometimes wonders what to make of the world," is really no improvement on "I sometimes wonder … " If the objective is to avoid using the first person, this kind of sentence should not even be attempted.

When using ratios such as one in ten, there can be confusion over plurality. Strictly speaking, it is correct to say "one in ten children are fat" because the children being described comprise a tenth of the population. But if the phrase is written "one child in five … " it is obviously correct to conclude … "is fat."

one-eighty   Recent rephrasing of 'U-turn' for a complete reversal of direction. It is a contraction of '180 degrees.'

on message   Fading slang for 'loyal,' from the days of electronic messaging devices by which employees, members of parliament etc could be contacted by managers.

onomatopoeia   Figure of speech for words that imitate the sounds of the action they describe, as in 'snap' and 'crackle.' Greek *onomatopoiia* (word-making).

onside   Recent adverb formed by contracting 'on the same side' and meaning 'in agreement' as, "the Prime Minister was insistent his colleagues should be onside where European unification was concerned."

on to   Writing this as a one-word preposition, onto, is widespread but still not correct in British English.

-ony   This suffix means the word refers to identification, from its Greek root, *onoma* (name). Thus, an anonym is a person or object with no name – Greek *a* (not) – and synonym is a word with the same meaning as another – Greek *sun* (together).

Opposites   A simple and enjoyable game that can do much to extend the vocabulary of young children. The quizmaster gives the keyword and the participants try to be first to name its opposite. With younger children, the elementary words below will provide a starting point, progressing to the more advanced suggestions at a later stage. Of course, there are very often several equally appropriate opposites to the word in question, so quizmasters must be flexible.

Elementary level:

above – below/under
accept – refuse/reject
add – subtract/take away
ahead – behind
always – never
arrive – depart
asleep – awake
beginning – end
behind – in front
blunt – sharp
brave – cowardly
bright – dim
busy – idle
buy – sell
cold – hot

cool – warm
come – go
dark – light
dead – alive
deep – shallow
down – up
east – west
easy – difficult/hard
entrance – exit
everything – nothing
far – near
fast – slow
forward – back
friend – enemy
friendly – hostile
gain – lose
gentle – rough

give – take
good – bad
hello – goodbye
hit – miss
home – away
in – out
innocent – guilty
join – separate
joy – sorrow
late – early
less – more
light – dark
long – short
love – hate
mean – generous
multiply – divide
night – day
noise – silence
north – south

optician

numerous – few
often – seldom
open – shut
oppose – support
past – future
polite – rude
poor – rich
positive – negative
quick – slow
rise – fall
rough – smooth
sad – happy
safe – dangerous
sense – nonsense
short – tall
shut – open
soft – hard
start – finish/stop
strong – weak
tame – wild
thin – thick
together – apart
true – false
under – over
valiant – cowardly
war – peace
wet – dry
win – lose
young – old

Advanced level:
abstain – indulge
abundance – scarcity/shortage
adept – inept
adopt – disown
acute – chronic/mild
acquire – relinquish
advance – retire
afloat – aground
amateur – professional
assemble – disperse
calm – frantic
compliment – insult
dearth – glut
exaggeration – understatement
expand – contract
extend – abbreviate
fierce – timid
fleeting – eternal/permanent
forbid – allow/permit
foreign – native
haphazard –

deliberate
hardline – moderate
harmony – discord
heretic – conformist
homogeneous – heterogeneous
hostile – friendly
imaginary – real
natural – artificial/synthetic
neutral – biased
nocturnal – diurnal
novice – expert/veteran
objective – subjective
oriental – occidental
plenty – want
progress – regress
reveal – conceal
sacred – profane
stubborn – flexible
synonym – antonym
wilful – biddable/obedient
zenith – nadir

optician A person who prescribes and provides spectacles or contact lenses. Distinct from an ophthalmologist, a person medically qualified to diagnose and treat disorders of the eye.

organic It describes a worldwide movement to grow crops and breed livestock without resorting to the use of inorganic chemicals such as synthetic fertilisers, pesticide, herbicides and fungicides. The principal objective is to minimize damage to the environment, but there are claims, too, that food from organically cultivated crops and livestock are healthier to eat. In chemistry, 'organic' can be quite narrowly defined as anything containing carbon. But in the context of food production, organic is much less easily determined. Many nations have voluntary or semi-official bodies that licence the use of the description organic, but there is by no means a universal standard. Greek *organon* (tool).

ordinance and **ordnance**   An ordinance is an official decree or order, as, "this park is closed under local authority ordinance." Ordnance is a collective word for military weaponry, as in "the battalion has expended an enormous amount of ordnance."

ortho-   Words with this prefix denote straightness, directness and genuineness, as in an orthodontist, who straightens teeth, or orthodox behaviour, which does not waver from the normal. Greek *orthos* (upright).

Orthodox   When referring to the churches of, for example, Greece and Russia, use the initial capital, as in the Greek Orthodox Church.

out   Recent verb formation claimed by the homosexual community. To 'out' someone known (or presumed) to be an unadmitted homosexual is to make their sexuality widely known, usually against their will. The new verb has already come into wider use as, for example, 'outing' individual celebrities as fans of despised pop musicians or football clubs.

overclass   Recent ironic adoption from 'underclass' to describe any privileged elite.

Oxford comma   A curiosity, this describes the optional final comma before the conjunction at the conclusion of a list. "Red, white, and blue" has the Oxford comma. "Red, white and blue" does not.

Oxford English   Yet another way of saying standard, received, or unaccented English.

Oxford English Dictionary   The first comprehensive dictionary of the English language, the first edition was begun in the 1850s, but

oxymoron

not completed until 1928. The full dictionary, in many volumes, is in a continuous state of updating, and its main editions are supplemented by regular new editions of the *Shorter Oxford* and *Concise Oxford* dictionaries, as well as many other supporting reference works.

oxymoron   Figure of speech in which the component parts of a phrase appear to contradict each other, as in 'debtbuster loan' and 'devout sceptic.' Greek *oxus* (sharp) and *moros* (foolish).

P

paean and **paeon** A paean is a song of praise or triumph – so the phrase 'paeans of praise' is a tautology – and a paeon is a term from prosody (*qv*) for a metrical foot comprising three short syllables and one long one. The words share the same Greek root, *Paian*, the Homeric name for the physician who attended the gods. The word peon, for a labourer in Mexico and other former Spanish-speaking American nations is rooted from Latin *pes*, meaning a foot, but is unrelated.

paed- Prefix meaning child, from Greek *paid-* (of a child or boy), gives us the word paediatrics, the branch of medicine concerned with children, but also the sinister and now widely used word paedophile, meaning a criminal sexually obsessed with children.

palate Beware confused use of this word, meaning the roof of the mouth and thus the sense of taste. A palette is a different thing, namely an artist's board for carrying and mixing paints. A pallet is yet another different thing – or several different things – a bed, a craftsman's implement or a type of liftable wooden platform for bearing bulky loads.

pallet See palate

palette See palate.

palindrome Figure of speech in which a word or phrase reads the same when written backwards or forwards, as in "Madam, I'm Adam." Greek *palin* (again) and *drom* (run).

Panglossian Eponym (word formed from someone's name) for the nature or pronouncements of an unwarrantedly optimistic person, from fictional Dr Pangloss in Voltaire's satire *Candide* of 1759. Philosopher Pangloss held that all is for the best in the best of all possible worlds, even amidst the cruelties and indignities he suffered in the novel – which itself ridicules the theory of a God-given harmony between man's spirit and the material world propounded by German Enlightenment philosopher Gottfried Leibniz.

pantomime   Originally a Roman dumb-show in which actors mimed instead of speaking – from Greek *pantomimos* (imitator of all). This drama form in the 21st century is now, in Britain, a popular and voluble children's entertainment, and one of the last branches of theatre to have enduring appeal to younger audiences. The plays are largely adaptations of the fairy tales written by Frenchman Charles Perrault in the 17th century. His 'Perrault's Popular Tales', first published in English by translator Andrew Lang in 1888, include *Blue Beard*, *Cinderella*, *Mother Goose*, *Puss in Boots*, *Red Riding Hood* and *Sleeping Beauty*.

pants   The first use of the phrase 'a pile of pants' to dismiss any object of contempt has been credited to BBC Radio One disc jockey Simon Mayo around 1990. Now shortened merely to 'pants' the term has become firmly established in vernacular British English. It does, at least, obviate the need for more abusive or indecent terminology.

paparazzo   This eponym, from the name of a character in Frederico Fellini's 1960 film *La Dolce Vita*, is set to prosper in the 21st century just as well as it did in the 20th. As in the movie original, it characterises a type of (usually freelance) photographer who pursues celebrities – often in the packs known collectively as paparazzi.

para-   Words beginning with this prefix are determined in three principal ways. The commonest are the two conflicting senses of closeness and distance, from the Greek *para* meaning either beside or beyond – as in parallel, meaning alongside one another or as in paramedic, meaning distanced from a true medic (doctor), but nevertheless analogous to one. The third sense of para- is from French origins and means protecting against, as in parasol, giving protection against the sun or parachute, giving protection against falling too fast. Many words in English starting with the letters p-a-r-a are, however, not rooted in either the Greek or the French prefix. An example is paraffin, from Latin *parum* (little) and *affinis* (having affinity).

parable   A story told to illustrate a moral lesson, as the parable of the good Samaritan, one of many such narratives recorded in the New Testament. Latin parabole (comparing).

paradigm   Very much a 21st-century buzz word, a paradigm (pronounced PARA dime) is nothing more than a model or example, as "Parliament in Westminster is sometimes seen as a paradigm for democratic government around the world." The term 'paradigm shift,' meaning a fundamental change in belief or direction, has already become an embarrassing cliché and should be avoided.

   Paradigm is also a term in grammar, describing all the inflected forms of a word, as the paradigm of the pronoun 'I' is 'I, me, mine, myself.' Greek *paradeiknunai* (to display side by side).

paragraph   A fundamental skill in writing readable English is the effective use of paragraphs. There are no rules, but it makes obvious sense to allow the reader regular pauses and divisions in any written work. In popular newspapers, paragraphs are commonly restricted to no more than one sentence each. Even in loftier papers, sub-editors are inclined to keep paragraphs to no more than three. The use of paragraphs is a discipline on the writer as well as a service to the reader. It makes you order your thoughts and to avoid overdeveloping single topics or ideas.

parallel   Unusually, the verb to parallel does not take a double 'l' when suffixed – so it is spelled 'paralleled' unlike the form in cancelled, parcelled, travelled etc.

parameter   This annoying buzz word's original, mathematical sense is explained in the Oxford dictionaries as "a quantity constant in the case considered but varying in different cases." The connection with the present general meaning of "limitation" for parameter is impossible to fathom. Avoid.

paraphrase   To express the same idea in different words, or to adapt a given phrase to a new context, as in "to paraphrase Oscar Wilde, 'I have nothing to declare but my genius'."

parenthesis   Figure of speech in which a comment or explanation is dropped into a sentence, as in "the mother-in-law –

parsing

God help us – is coming to stay." The parenthesis may be defined by dashes, commas or the brackets known as parentheses.

parsing   Lost art of identifying all the components of a text, and once one of the fundamental exercises that tested and informed pupils in English. To parse a phrase such as "man bites dog" involves noting that the singular noun 'man' is the subject of the sentence, the verb 'bites' is the third person singular of the present tense of the verb to bite, and the singular noun 'dog' is the object of the sentence.

participle   Type of word formed from a verb. There are two kinds, present participle and past participle. The present participle of 'to do' is 'doing' and the past participle is 'done.'

partner   As traditional marriage retreats, partner is replacing husband/wife. New words emerge in the wake of the trend. 'Unpartnered' is a common substitute for 'unmarried' in defining a person living alone.

parts of speech   The phrase sounds old-fashioned now, recalling as it does an era of English-teaching in which the language was analysed in much more fragmented detail than it is today. But a basic understanding of the parts of speech (and equally written English) is surely as useful in the 21st century as at any other time. The said parts are the nine defined types of words:

1.   Articles – a, the etc
2.   Nouns – apple, beauty etc
3.   Pronouns – I, she etc
4.   Verbs – aspire, betray etc
5.   Adjectives – angry, brutal etc
6.   Adverbs – angrily, brutally etc
7.   Prepositions – at, beyond etc
8.   Conjunctions – and, but etc
9.   Interjections – ah!, bother! etc

Grammarians (teachers) group parts of speech according to whether they are 'content' words or 'function' words. Content words are nouns, verbs, adjectives and adverbs. Function words account for all the rest, so known because their function extends only to demonstrating the meaning of content words, rather than conveying any meaning of their own. Some teachers use the collective terms 'form class' for content words and 'structure class' for function words.

passive   In grammar, the 'voice' of a verb. See active and passive.

passed and **past**   Passed is the past participle of the verb to pass. Past is either a noun meaning the time before the present, or an adjective meaning former.

peculiar   The word has two distinct meanings. There is the familiar sense of weird or strange, as in "his behaviour is very peculiar," but also the sense of set apart or individualistic, as in "he has a peculiar talent."

peddler or **pedlar**   In British English, use pedlar.

phatic   Recent (1920s) word for the language used in communication between strangers to acknowledge each other rather than to convey anything, as in one person at a bus stop saying to another, "nice day, isn't it?." Greek *phatos* (spoken).

phenomenon   This is strictly the singular form of the word, as in "soccer phenomenon Wayne Rooney." Phenomena is the plural, as in "dangerous weather phenomena."

-phile   Words with this suffix refer to love – or at least fondness. An anglophile is an admirer of England and/or the English. In a more sinister context, a paedophile is a criminal with an unnatural obsession with young children. Greek *philos* (loving).

philology   The scientific study of the origins, development and use of language.

philosophy   The original Ancient Greek word, *philosophia*, meant 'love of wisdom' and this is still a reasonable translation for the 21st century. Philosophy as a 'science' has spawned an academic industry in which the writings of philosophers from the first Greeks – Socrates, Plato and so on – up to the British philosophers of the modern era – Russell, Wittgenstein *et al* – are studied, interpreted and reinterpreted. The intentions and functions of philosophy are, of course, as much obscured by the limitations of vocabulary as they are illuminated by the millions of

phoneme

words devoted to their explanation. On the one hand, what words can possibly be adequate to describe the Meaning of Life? On the other hand, what better use can there be for words than to describe the Meaning of Life? These and countless other questions of philosophy will no doubt continue to be talked and written about for as long as we have words to expend on them.

phoneme   In speech, a unit of sound. In the world of literacy-teaching, phoneme is a buzz word, used by educationists to elevate what was once called a 'word sound' into a more scientific-sounding term. Britain's National Curriculum for children aged five to seven, for example, specifies they should be taught to "hear, identify, segment and blend phonemes in words." This sort of jargon, of course, makes the comprehension of the bases of literacy just that little bit harder for teachers to communicate, and young children to understand. The English language is said to comprise 42 principal phonemes. Greek *phoneo* (I speak).

PIE   An acronym beloved of philologists (those who study the evolution of languages), it stands for Proto-Indo-European. It's the name given to the language believed to have been spoken around 5,000 years ago by people living on the northern shores of the Black Sea at the southeastern edge of Europe, and extending into Asia as far as northern India. These tribes subsequently migrated westwards into northern Europe where their way of speaking evolved into what we now call Germanic languages, and also into southern Europe, where the same process led to the formation of the Greek and then the Latin languages. Modern European languages, including English, are evolved from these origins.

pikey   Recent term of contempt for members of the underclass, formerly more identified with gypsies than at present.

pittance   Beware this word. It is now commonly used to mean a miserly sum, as in "they pay her a pittance for working round the clock." But a pittance is really a gift, as originally given via local subscription to a poor monastery or priory to provide a little extra comfort, usually to mark the anniversary of the death of the order's founder or some other saint's day or festival. So a pittance symbolises not meanness, but a type of generosity now lost in the era of state welfare-provision. The word comes from Latin *pietas*, root of English 'piety', and meaning both loving kindness and the respect in which we hold (or should hold) our ancestors. It is also the source of 'Pieta' the name given to depictions of the dead Christ cradled by his mother the Virgin Mary, such as the great sculpture by Michaelangelo in the Vatican.

place names   In Britain, let alone worldwide, there are plenty of place names that are chronically misspelled, often because their pronunciation seems at such a distance from their suggested phonetic sound. Examples are Leominster (pronounced 'Lemster') and Wisbech (pronounced 'Wizbeech). Other names, with more than one word or incorporating the names of the rivers upon which they stand, present difficulties over hyphens. Here are some of the most frequent offenders, spelled or punctuated as they should be.

Accrington (Lancashire)
Aldeburgh (Suffolk)
Alnwick (Northumberland)
Ashby-de-la-Zouch (Leicestershire)
Betws-y-Coed (Gwynedd)
Bicester (Oxfordshire)
Bideford (Devon)
Bradford-on-Avon (Wiltshire)
Bridgwater (Somerset)
Caernarfon (Gwynedd)
Castle Cary (Somerset)
Chester-le-Street (Durham)
Crieff (Tayside)
Cupar (Fife)
Denbigh (Clwyd)
Ellesmere Port (Cheshire)
Ffestiniog (Gwynedd)
Fowey (Cornwall)
Frome (Somerset)

Guildford (Surrey)
Inveraray (Strathclyde)
Kirkcudbright (Dumfries & Galloway)
Leamington Spa (Warwickshire)
Leek (Staffordshire)
Leicester (Leicestershire)
Leominster (Hereford & Worcester)
Lichfield (Staffordshire)
Llanelli (Dyfed)
Looe (Cornwall)
Malmesbury (Gloucestershire)
Middlesborough (Cleveland)
Musselburgh (Lothian)
Newcastle upon Tyne (Tyne & Wear)
Okehampton (Devon)
Reigate (Surrey)

Rhondda (Glamorgan)

Rhyl (Clwyd)

Rippon (Yorkshire)

Shepton Mallet (Somerset)

Stranraer (Dumfries &
 Galloway)

Stoke-on-Trent
 (Staffordshire)

Stratford-upon-Avon
 (Wawickshire)

Sutton Coldfield (Birmingham)

Tameside (Greater
 Manchester)

Teignmouth (Devon)

Tewkesbury (Gloucestershire)

Thame (Oxfordshire)

Thurso (Highland)

Tonbridge (Kent)

Tunbridge Wells (Kent)

Uttoxeter (Staffordshire)

Wallasey (Merseyside)

Ware (Hertfordshire)

Welwyn Garden City
 (Hertfordshire)

Weston-super-Mare
 (Somerset)

Winchelsea (East Sussex)

Wisbech (Cambridgeshire)

Wrexham (Clwyd)

Yeovil (Somerset)

plagiarism Intentionally passing off someone else's written work as your own. Latin *plagiarus* (kidnapper).

Plain English Campaign A well-intentioned commercial body describing itself as "an independent pressure group fighting for public information to be written in plain English."

plain sailing This is the correct version now, but the phrase was 'plane sailing' until about 200 years ago.

plant names In writing botanical plant names, give an initial capital to the genus (botanical category) but not to the species (individual member of the genus). Thus, the 300 or so species of pinks and carnations are all known as *Dianthus* and variously as *Dianthus alpinus*, *Dianthus chinensis* etc. Use italics for these Latin names in typed work. Many modern plant species are identified not by a Latin botanical species name, but after an individual or other proper name. The correct way to write these is to put the genus as before, but add the species name in quotation marks, using initial capitals, as *Dianthus* 'Mrs Sinkins' and *Dianthus* 'Show Beauty.'

Platonic Referring to the Greek philosopher Plato (427–347 BC), it should be written with the initial capital. This applies also to the phrase 'Platonic love,' which continues to mean the transcending form of love described by Plato. Avoid using the term in a general sense to describe a relationship in which sex does not figure.

pluperfect tense   In grammar the tense of a verb describing an action that took place before a subsequent action described in the same sentence. In "he had gone before she arrived" the verb 'had gone' is the pluperfect tense of 'to go'. Latin *plus quam perfectum* (more than perfect).

plural   Numbering more than one. In grammar, the plural form is, obviously enough, usually made by adding the letter 's' or letters 'es, ses, tes' etc. The plural forms of many words follow those of the words they derive from, as 'phenomena' as plural of 'phenomenon.'

political correctness   So-called after American politicians' habit of mincing their words in hope of offending the fewest possible voters in racial, religious or other minorities, this late-20th-century social phenomenon continues to have a significant influence on the language. It is often shortened to PC. Arbiters of political correctness have declared many apparently innocent words and phrases injurious to the sensibilities of certain sections of the community, especially women, racial groups, the disabled and elderly. In instinctive response, journalists and comedians ridicule the trend, coining ever-sillier new terms as gross caricatures – only to find their inventions adopted without a trace of irony into the jargon of officialdom. Following are some of the alleged offenders, with the charges laid against them, and a few of the words campaigners (or disbelieving commentators) have suggested as acceptable substitutes:

animal – not to be used to describe behaviour of football hooligans etc. Demeans animal species.

bald – may offend those without hair. Use balding, receding, thinning – or, jocularly (but still politically correct) follically challenged.

black – may offend people from certain racial backgrounds if used in pejorative context: black art, blackball, black-hearted, black look etc.

political correctnes

blind – may offend people without sight. Use visually impaired.

chairman – excludes women. Replace with chair or chairperson.

crazy – *see* mad.

drunk – offensive to alcoholics. Use either tired or emotional, or both.

dustman – demeans refuse collectors (especially female).

fat – may offend overweight people. Alternative suggestions include big, generous, larger.

gentleman – members of some socio-economic groups may infer their own exclusion and take offence.

halfwit – *see* mad.

history – excludes women.

housewife – demeans women, especially those unmarried.

lady – members of some socio-economic groups may infer their own exclusion and take offence.

lunatic – *see* mad.

mad – offends mental patients, their families and carers. Replace with suffering from learning difficulties.

mankind – excludes women. Replace with humankind.

nitty-gritty – this vernacular synonym for 'brass tacks' as in 'getting down to ... ' has been proscribed by one further education college. The premise is that it once denoted sexual union between black slaves and white slave owners and is therefore offensive to some racial groups.

normal couple – could be deemed to exclude unmarried or homosexual couples.

ratcatcher – demeans ratcatchers. Use rodent operative.

sex change – may offend people undergoing the experience. Use gender redesignation.

shirtlifter – may offend homosexual people.

short – may offend people below average height. Replace with petite (females only).

slaving over a hot stove – trivialises plight of former slaves.

stewardess – demeans female airline staff. Use flight attendant.

taking the mickey – offends Irish people.

working class – may offend members of some socio-economic groups.

poly-   Prefix denoting many, as in 'polyglot,' a speaker of many languages. Greek *polloi* (many).

pore and **pour**   To pore is to be intent on or absorbed by study, especially of a book, as "she spent years poring over ancient manuscripts. To pour is to dispense a drink, as in "he poured her a cup of tea."

pornography   In the Ancient Greek original, it was the 'writing of harlots' from *porne* (prostitute) and *graphos* (writing). Now a portrayal in any medium intended or inferred to arouse a sexual response more than an aesthetic one. In law, pornography has been defined as any material with a tendency to deprave or corrupt, but criteria vary widely throughout the world. The impact of the word has been eroded by its use against even mildly titillating material which affronts the taste, rather than the morals, of the audience. 'Hard-core' and 'soft-core' are now used to distinguish between more- or less-offensive varieties of pornography.

Portakabin   Trade mark.

portmanteau words   are formed by blending all or part of two existing words. A portmanteau, from French, is a type of travelling bag opening up into two equal halves. The name was first used for blends such as 'chortle' (to laugh gleefully, from chuckle and snort) created by author Lewis Carroll (1832–98). Portmanteau words in current use include agitprop (agitation and propaganda), alcopop (alcohol and pop), animatronic (animated and electronic), brunch (breakfast and lunch), camcorder (camera and recorder), docudrama (documentary and drama), electrocute (electro- and execute), emoticon (emote and icon), faction (fact and fiction), fanzine (fan and magazine), gazunder (gazump and under), glitterati (glitter and literati), guesstimate (guess and estimate), infotainment (information and entertainment), moped (motor and pedal), motel (motor and hotel), motorcade (motor and cavalcade), Oxbridge (Oxford and Cambridge), palimony (pal and alimony), pixel (picture and element), pulsar (pulse and quasar), smog (smoke and fog), squirearchy (squire and hierarchy), squirl (squiggle and twirl), stagflation (stagnation and inflation), telegenic (television and photogenic), trafficator

possessive

(traffic and indicator), transistor (transfer and resistor), widget (wizard and gadget), workaholic (work and alcoholic), yatter (yammer or yap and chatter), yonks (years, months, weeks).

possessive   In grammar, the case of nouns and pronouns denoting ownership. In "Whose is this?" 'whose' is the possessive case of 'who.' Same as genitive case. The possessive pronouns are: my, your, his, her, its, our and their. The absolute forms are mine, yours, his, hers, its, ours and theirs.

post-   The prefix denotes the meaning 'after' in many words, as in 'post-war.' Latin post (after).

postmodern   Annoying buzz word. Note one word without a hyphen. There is no consensus as to what the word means. One definition by a newspaper writer in 2002: "the blurring between what is considered high and low art." Strictly speaking, it means after or beyond what is recent or current, but it does not mean futuristic.

potboiler   A novel written for no better reason than to earn the writer a living – at least to the extent of financing the fuel to keep the cooker running. The term is more recently used by critics to describe a story that has little literary merit but holds the attention. This may well be a confusion with 'pageturner.'

pour   See pore.

practice and **practise**   In British English, 'practice' is the noun, as in "a doctor's practice," and 'practise' is the verb, as in "she practises medicine."

precis   A summary of a speech or text. From French précis, but in English now written without the acute accent.

predicate   In grammar, it's a noun meaning the part of a sentence that describes the action taken by the subject. So, in 'man bites dog' 'man' is the subject and 'bites dog' is the predicate. As a verb in grammar, to predicate is to assert something about the subject of a sentence. Latin *prae* (beforehand) and *dicare* (to make known).

pre-emptive etc   All words formed by the prefix pre- before an initial letter e – pre-eminent, pre-exist etc – should be written with a hyphen.

preface   a statement preceding the main text of a book. Authors describe their methods and motives, apologise for shortcomings or inveigh against all the difficulties strewn in a writer's path. In a telling passage from an unpublished preface to his great, introspective poem *Endymion*, John Keats had this to say:

"In a great nation, the work of an individual is of so little importance; his pleadings and excuses are so uninteresting; his 'way of life' such a nothing; that a preface seems a sort of impertinent bow to strangers who care nothing about it."

prefix   The first section of a word, hyphenated or not, that modifies the sense, as in the migration of meaning between 'wife' and 'ex-wife' or 'normal' and 'subnormal.'

prehistoric   It's one word – no hyphen. The term refers to the time before history, which means the time before human beings kept either pictographic or written records. That accounts for all of time except the last 10,000 years or so.

premise   An assumption made for the purpose of reasoning; as, an argument based on a false premise. Formerly also 'premiss' but this spelling is now rare. The plural premises, for a building and in particular a pub (as in licensed premises), has a connected meaning through its reference to a place from which one sets out. Latin *pre* (before) and *mittere* (to send).

preposition   Part of speech used to place a noun or pronoun in relationship to the rest of the sentence. 'She held the umbrella *over* the child to shelter him *from* the rain.' From Latin *prae*, in front of, and *positio*, placing. These are some of the words commonly used as prepositions: about, above, after, along, around, at, away, before, beside, between, beyond, by, down, for, from, in, into, near, of, on, out, over, to, under, up, upon, with, within, without.

It is a widely quoted 'rule' of Correct English that a sentence should not be ended with a preposition. The mystery is why such a convention has ever arisen, because there are many instances where a phrase or sentence concluding in such a way is unavoidable without obvious contrivance. There is no good reason not to say, for example, 'please sit down' or 'what is this all about?' or 'I felt he was someone I could rely on.' None of these phrases can be usefully altered by repositioning the preposition. Some writers have claimed that the English poet and classicist John Dryden (1631–1700) imported the rule into English from Latin, but this surely exaggerates the influence one individual can have on the language. Sir Winston Churchill commented with characteristic acuity on a sentence in a state document painfully worded in avoidance of a prepositional ending: 'This is the sort of English up with which I will not put.'

prescribe and **proscribe**   To prescribe is to recommend or lay down authoritatively, as a doctor prescribes a drug or a period of rest. To proscribe is to denounce or forbid, as a government proscribes a political enemy or that political enemy's activities.

present   In grammar, the tense of a verb describing the progress of an action taking place now. In "he is here" the verb 'is' is the present tense of 'to be'.

presenteeism   Recent ironic adoption from 'absenteeism' to describe the habit of being conspicuously at work during and beyond office hours, in hope (notoriously forlorn) of attracting the favourable attention of an employer.

pretension   Commonly misspelt word. Unlike the rule of attention from attend, intention from intend etc, the noun takes the 's.' The root of the word is from the later Latin form of *tensere* (earlier *tendere*), meaning to stretch. Dissension from dissent is another exception.

principal/principle   As an adjective, principal means foremost or leading, as in "money was her principal motivator." As a noun, principal means the head of an institution, as in "the college principal," or in finance, a capital sum, as in "he spent the interest but preserved the principal." Principle is a noun only, and principally means a basic truth or law, as in "stealing was against his principles."

pristine   Buzz word correctly describes something old that is perfectly preserved, just as if it had been newly made, as in "the Dinky toy was 50 years old but had never been removed from its box, and was in pristine condition." Pristine should not be used to describe something that looks new when it actually is new. Latin *pristinus* (former).

program and **programme** Program is the correct spelling in the context of computer software, but in British English use programme otherwise, as in programme of events, TV programme etc.

pronoun A pronoun is a word that stands in the place of a noun. The most familiar are the personal pronouns: I, you, he, she, it, we and they in the nominative or subjective, and me, you, him, her, it, us and them in the accusative or objective. Other pronouns are grouped under the descriptions 'reflexive' as in myself, yourself etc, 'demonstrative' as in this, that, these and those, and 'indefinite' as in any, each, none etc. See also interrogative and possessive pronouns.

pronunciation 'Correct' pronunciation as defined in English dictionaries is 'Received Standard' English, sometimes informally called Oxford English, really meaning English as spoken in southern England. Thus, the *Concise Oxford Dictionary* states that 'bath' is pronounced with a long 'ah' sound, without mentioning the common alternative pronunciation with a short 'a' as in 'bat.' Neither pronunciation, of course, is more correct than the other – any more than one regional accent is preferable to another.

But some words do have disputed pronunciations unconnected to regional influences. A well-known example is 'controversy.' Is it KON troh versy or kon TROV ersy? Dictionaries do little to settle the controversy, preferring to give both pronunciations. Their commitment to one or other pronunciation goes no further than a mention in their introductory sections that the first one stated has been deemed (by no stated authority) to be the more commonly used.

propaganda A derogatory word for information spread by politically or idealogically undesirable individuals or groups, as, depending on your point of view, Nazi propaganda or White House propaganda. When trying to write from a balanced

proper nouns

standpoint, use the word propaganda with care. It originates from the Latin name of a Vatican committee of cardinals charged with spreading the Roman Catholic faith overseas, the *congregatio de propaganda fide*.

proper nouns   In grammar, this old-fashioned term describes any person, place, brand or other specific item that is customarily written with an initial capital letter, as in James, Newcastle or Microsoft.

proscribe   See prescribe.

prose   Written work as distinguished from poetry.

prosody   In language, especially poetry, the structure that gives the written work its sounds and rhythms. The many strange terms used to deconstruct verse – dactyls and spondees, alexandrines and hexameters – are all from the vocabulary of prosody. Greek *prosodia* (song to music).

protagonist   Originally the principal role in a drama, but now used to mean just about any leading person at the centre of events, real or imaginary. Greek *protos* (first) and *agonistes* (actor).

Protestant   It seems astounding that one arm of the Christian faith continues to describe itself in perpetual protest at the beliefs and customs of the old doctrine, Catholicism, 500 years after Dutch scholar-priest Erasmus's criticisms of the Roman church launched the Reformation. But many communities worldwide, not just Northern Ireland, are split into these distinct sects. Use the initial capital for Protestants – and Catholics.

protester or **protestor**   Both are current, but protester is more rational.

proto-   Words with this prefix commonly denote the action of being first, as in 'prototype,' a first version.

proverb   A familiar saying that conveys a basic truth, as in "time waits for no man." Not the same as a cliché, but nevertheless use with discretion.

pseudonym   Name assumed especially by authors, as John Le Carré, spy-thriller writer, is the pseudonym of former intelligence officer David Cornwell. Greek *pseudos* (deception) and *onoma* (name).

psychological novel   The first novels to explore the workings of characters' minds did not appear until the second half of the 19th century. Anthony Trollope was a pioneer, and Leo Tolstoy a great master. Today, just about all literary novels are psychological to some degree.

publication titles   Newspapers and periodicals should always be correctly identified by their 'masthead' titles – the names exactly as they appear on their front pages. So it's *The Times* and *The Daily Telegraph* but the *Daily Mail* and the *Daily Mirror*. In typed work, it is customary to use italics to identify titles.

punctuation   The stops and commas of English punctuation come to us from Greek writings of at least five hundred years BC, when their antecedents were used in scripts prepared for the chorus in ritual and, later, drama. See under the various marks for more detailed accounts.

purdah   In the general sense, an enforced seclusion, as the perpetrator of a major social gaffe might find himself 'in purdah' through shunning by his friends. Originally, it is the word in both Persian and Urdu for a curtain behind which women in a household would be concealed from male eyes – and thus, metaphorically, the whole condition of women living in seclusion.

Purgatory   Not to be confused with Hell. In Roman Catholic tradition, Purgatory is a staging point for the souls of the dead. On their way to Heaven, they are purged of their venial (forgivable) sins. Write purgatory in lower case when using it metaphorically, as in 'the holiday was sheer purgatory.' Latin *purgare*, to purify.

Q

QED It stands for *quad erat demonstrandum*, Latin for 'that was to be demonstrated.'

qua this annoying word is a favourite with the more-ruthless type of Scrabble player. Unknown to most of us, it means 'in the capacity of', being the adverbial ablative of Latin *qui*, meaning who. Note that it is the feminine gender and that, strictly speaking, it would be correct in the phrase "the Queen qua Defender of the Faith" but incorrect in "Prince Philip qua Queen's Consort."

quantum From the language of physics, this word has been borrowed for the strange phrase 'quantum leap' to describe any unexpected and large advance in activity – usually intellectual or technological. Within physics, a quantum is a defined measure of energy existing in one form or another. Its definition is established by its smallness – a quantum is indivisible and usually subatomic (smaller than an atom) and its leap (or jump) is an apparent transition from, for example, particle form to wave form.

The lay media seems to relish reference to the quantum world. "About as easy to understand as quantum mechanics" is a typical jocular description of any kind of perplexing topic. But quantum mechanics – derived from the quantum theory of German physicist Max Planck first made public in 1901 – is a hugely important branch of science and is behind many of the greatest advances of the last 100 years.

quasi It means 'almost' or 'as it were' as, in the notorious semi-official committee known as a quango, standing for quasi non-governmental organisation. Latin *quasi* (as if).

Quattrocento A pivotal period in Italian art of the Renaissance, it describes not the 14th century, but the hundred years from 1401 to 1500.

Queen In reference to the present British monarch, always u̲ the initial capital, but write as 'the Queen' not 'The Queen.'

question mark Represented by ? it is used at the end of all interrogative sentences. The one difficulty can be deciding whether a sentence is interrogative or not. "Would you like an apple?" is plainly interrogative, but "Would you kindly get out of my way," is more of a request than a question. The best method when writing down this sort of dialogue is to say it to yourself out loud. If it's supposed to sound like a question, finish it with a question mark. If it isn't, don't.

Quiller-Couch, Arthur See 'murder your darlings.'

quite One of those words to which usage can give almost contrary meaning. A drama critic who describes a performance as "quite brilliant" means it is entirely or utterly brilliant. But a play reviewed as "quite good" is being dismissed as less-than good, possibly even bad. As a term of agreement, quite (in earlier times quite so) is simply a synonym for exactly.

In reporting and reviewing, it is fine to quote from what other writers or reporters have written, provided you do so in a direct way, and identifying the quotation by setting it apart or enclosing it in quotation marks. If the quote is more than a few words, it is a courtesy to add where the quotation comes from, by noting the name of the book or other publication.

quotation marks Double or single? Strict rules do not exist, but consistency is important. Newspapers and periodicals tend to favour double quotes for direct speech and single quotes for nominated items, but book publishers commonly use single quotes for both. Where a quotation occurs within direct speech, use the alternative form, thus: "He asked me, 'Do you come here often?' and I told him, 'No, I don't.' "

qv Referencing device, as used frequently in this book. Abbreviation for *quod vide*, Latin for 'which see.'

R

rack and **wrack**   The spelling 'rack' is now used in all senses except for the seaweed called wrack. So it's "rack and ruin," "plate rack," "on the rack," "racking my brains," and so on.

racquet   Stringed implement for badminton, squash and tennis – or the now near-extinct court game of racquets. From French *racquette* after Arabic *raha* (palm of the hand) and distinct from racket, a word imitative of a noise or disturbance. Racquet is correct in the sporting context, but the spelling 'racket' is now at least as common in this sense. Dictionaries list racquet as a mere alternative to the other spelling, which seems a shame as a 'tennis racket' could, after all, equally refer to the sound of the Wimbledon crowds or an alleged fraud in the sport.

rainbow   Now adopted as a collective term for minority groups, originally racial, but now even more widely, as in 'a rainbow alliance' of feminists and gay rights activists against discrimination in employment or government policy.

rebarbative   This strange and much-misused word means repulsive, as in an unattractive person. It is originally French, derived from *barbe*, meaning a beard – a facial adornment worn as a religious observance in some faiths to render the wearer less alluring than he would be if clean-shaven.

receive   One of the most misspelt words in the language.

received pronunciation   English spoken without regional accent. In the 21st century, it is widely taken to be the English used by the upper class, including the royal family. But it is in fact the manner of speaking common to millions of people who for one reason or another lack an identifiable regional accent. Some linguists claim 'RP' dates from the 1920s and that its spread has been due mostly to the imitation of unaccented voices heard on radio and later, television. But from the 1980s, the standard or 'Oxford' English once expected of broadcasters has progressively given way to regionally accented voices, so that RP is now little heard outside the middle-class ghettos of BBC Radio 3 and 4. And many performers and presenters in television drama and entertainment now use a new form of London-based received pronunciation variously known as Estuary English, Mockney or Sarf London. Thus, media-addicted people – particularly the young – from all parts of the United Kingdom are tending to acquire their accented English not on a regional basis from their parents, neighbours or peers but from the speech of characters in Metropolitan television soap operas.

redundant   See tautology.

re-enter etc   All words formed by the prefix re- before an initial letter e – re-employ, re-examine etc – should be written with a hyphen.

referendum   It might be scholarly to write the plural of this Latin gerund as 'referenda,' but it can sound pretentious. Stick to referendums.

refrain   In poetry and song, a repeated phrase or lines.

regime   There is no longer any need to add the accent from the original French *régime*.

Register Office   Civil marriages in the United Kingdom can be conducted in an official Register Office. The term 'registry office' is incorrect.

regretful and **regrettable**   A person is regretful, as in 'she was regretful following the failure of her marriage.' An event or circumstance is regrettable, as in 'the failure of her marriage was regrettable.' Beware confusing the two.

reign   See rein.

rein   Beware misspelling this word as 'reign' as in "the East India Company ... attempted to reign in its junior employees" (*Spectator*, 2001). To rein in is to control, as with the bridle on a horse. To reign is to rule as a monarch.

Renaissance   It started in Italy in the late 14th century and was, as the word signifies, a 'rebirth' of secular culture after centuries of Catholic Church control over the arts, literature and even politics. The English Renaissance starts later, really with the end of the Wars of the Roses in 1485, when the Crown was recentralised and people could start to turn their energies to creativity rather than mere survival. The process was accelerated when Henry VIII (1509–47) loosened the grip of the Catholic Church, and stripped it of its monastic possessions and domination of art, music and literature.

Restoration A period in art and literature coinciding with the restoration of the English monarchy, in the person of King Charles II, in 1660.

Reverend The correct abbreviation is Revd, without a full point.

rhetoric The art of speaking or writing well. It's now an old-fashioned word, mostly heard in the phrase "empty rhetoric," meaning a wordy and pointless speech. Greek *rhetor* (speaker).

rhetorical question A question expressed more for effect than in expectation of a response, as in the despairing phrase 'who cares?' which really means 'I don't care.'

roman In typography, a plain, upright face as distinct from a script-style italic face. In this context, the word has no initial capital, but Roman otherwise should always be so spelt.

Roman numerals Even in the 21st century, Roman numerals persist in titles, as in Henry VIII and Elizabeth II, and in the dates still used by broadcasters and filmmakers, who seem to prefer MMV to 2005. The simplicity of such dates is one of the clear advantages of living in the early years of a new century.

round See around

RP See received pronunciation

S

saga   Once upon a time a saga was exclusively a medieval Nordic tale, but the meaning has long since been extended to a story told in episodes, often describing the events in the lives of successive generations of a family, as in John Galsworthy's popular *The Forsyte Saga* between 1906 and 1921. Now, there are television sagas, and a certain type of middle class novel is sneeringly known as an "aga saga."

sandal   Type of footwear. Note spelling is not 'sandle.'

saw   It means the same as a chestnut, but only in the context of a proverb or maxim, as in, "he gave us the old saw about the love of money being the root of all evil."

scapegoat   This strange word of Biblical origin – after a domestic goat upon which a Jewish priest would lay symbolic blame for all the sins of his flock and then despatch into the wilderness – is now in common use as a verb, as in "scapegoating parents for the sins of their children."

scenario   As well as being a plot outline for a play, scenario can also be a theoretical or imagined series of events, as in, "the worst-case scenario is that the plane will crash and we'll all be killed." This is fine, but do not use 'scenario' in place of 'situation,' as far too many writers now do. Greek *skene* (stage).

schlock   From Yiddish, it has long been used in American English to mean an inferior kind of merchandise. The word has lately come into wider use in the phrase 'schlock horror' for a cheap and revolting book or film.

Scots, Scotsman, Scottish and **Scotch**   The author is Scots-born, and I use this distinction as my platform to declare that Scots are the people of Scotland and their language. Scots can also be used to denote the nationality of people born in Scotland. A Scotsman is an adult male member of the population, and also a popular brand name for hotels, newspapers and so forth. Scottish describes the nationality of all things indigenous to Scotland. Scotch is the principal among all the world's whiskies. I can hardly bear to write down the word Scotchman. It is a Sassenach insult and to be used only from a place of great safety.

Scott, Sir Walter Scottish balladist, novelist and publisher (1771–1832) was the most widely read author of his day. Growing from his early translations of romantic German ballads, his own original, romantic rhymes – such as *The Lady of the Lake* (1810) – soon turned into some of the first British historical fiction, most of it under the collective title the *Waverley Novels*. Scott's influence on English literature has been very great, and his contribution to the language likewise – signposted by neologisms (*qv*) such as freelance, gruesome, picaresque, red-handed and stalwart. He has the further distinction of having brought into use what was once the longest word to be found in the *Oxford English Dictionary*: floccipaucinihilipilification. Its meaning purports to be 'the act of estimating being worthless.'

sea change Now a cliché for a great shift or variation in actions or opinions, as in "revulsion at the crime has brought about a sea change in the public's attitude to child abuse," it is a curiosity that this term, suitably enough, comes from a famous passage in William Shakespeare's play *The Tempest*, written around 1608:

> Full fathom five thy father lies;
> Of his bones are coral made:
> Those are pearls that were his eyes:
> Nothing of him that doth fade,
> But doth suffer a sea-change
> Into something rich and strange.

Second World War In British English, this is more commonly used than the mainly American World War Two (or II). Some publications have very recently begun to do without the initial capitals.

self deprecating In the sense of being modest about one's own achievement, the verb deprecate, meaning to speak against, is right, and the verb depreciate, meaning to diminish in value, is wrong.

semantics In linguistics (qv) it is the study of meaning in words. The fact that semantics is a detached sort of science has earned the term a rather disdainful use, with the phrase "mere semantics" used to mean something very similar to "empty words." Avoid.

semicolon It is a wonder that this punctuation mark has survived into the 21st century at all. Back in the 1930s, George Orwell – among the most influential English users in any century – declared "the semicolon is an unnecessary stop" and that he would henceforth write without using any.

But for the ordinary writer, the semicolon is surely still indispensable in its principal role, dividing two related but distinct phrases that cannot be successfully separated with a conjunction, a comma or a full stop. Germaine Greer, one of the more felicitous users of the language, provides a fine example: "Other countries use baffles and screens to preserve the quality of life for people and animals living within sight of motorways; Britain doesn't."

The printed semicolon is 500 years old, dating from the first printings of Greek and Roman classics by the pioneering Italian typesetter Aldo Manucci in the 1490s. The mark first appears in printed English in the late 1600s.

Today, when the comma (qv) is so much misused, a facility with the semicolon should bring credit on the user. Do not be persuaded it is old fashioned; it is as vital in conveying meaning as it has ever been.

semi-modal verbs These are the verbs 'dare', 'need' and 'used to' when employed in an auxiliary sense. While the phrase "she dared him to show his feelings" uses dare as a simple transitive verb, the phrase "she dared not show her own feelings" uses dare as a semi-modal verb, auxiliary to the verb show.

semiotics The search for symbolism, especially in language. The Italian academic and writer Umberto Eco (born 1932) is the leading 'semiotician' in the world and was formerly Professor of Semiotics at Turin University. His popular novel *The Name of the*

sensual and sensuous

Rose (1980), a detective thriller centred on a medieval monastery but owing much to the style and methods of the Sherlock Holmes stories, has been called the "complete semiotic book." Semiotics may or may not be a useful science – the impenetrable mystery is whether the symbolism invades language via writers or via readers – but it certainly affords much opportunity for the deconstruction of literature and other art forms. As such it is a harmless intellectual pursuit. It is said to owe its origins to a remark made by the historian Thomas Carlyle (1795–1881): "In every object there is infinite meaning." Greek *semeion* (sign).

sensual and **sensuous**   Beware confusing these two distinct words. Sensual describes the response of any of the senses to hedonistic or sexual stimulation. Sensuous describes the response of the senses to aesthetic stimulation.

sentence   In grammar, it is a collection of words expressing a complete idea or item of information. The first word has an initial capital letter and the whole thing ends with a full stop. There are, of course, very many more definitions and variations than this. Some grammarians like to say that a sentence is only a sentence if it incorporates at least three elements, namely subject, verb and object, as in "Cats eat fish." But this is silly. "Fish tastes good." is surely equally a sentence, even though it lacks an object. Sentences can be any length you like, but beware losing the reader's attention. More than one subordinate clause, and the eye and mind can wander. It is an axiom that short sentences are more reader-friendly than long ones. Bear it in mind.

sentiment and **sentimentality**   The meanings of these two words are different. Sentiment is a feeling, belief or opinion which may or may not be coloured by emotion. Sentimentality is the indulgence, or even weakness, of wallowing in emotionally worked-up feelings. To love one's dog is a sentiment, but to love one's dog believing it understands every word you say to it is sentimentality. Latin *sentire* to feel).

sermon   It symptomises the spirit of the age that the word sermon is now largely pejorative, signifying something very close to a harangue – as in a defensive teenager's plea to an overbearing parent: "don't give me another of your sermons." Even as an address from the pulpit, the traditional Biblical discourse is commonly an object of ridicule, and certainly not bolstered by clergy who post signs outside their churches announcing the likes of: "No sermon on Sunday. God be praised." Latin *sermo* (speech).

set-up As a noun – "what kind of set-up do you call this?" – hyphenate it.

sew To stitch with needle and thread, as distinct from to sow, as in planting or scattering seed.

sex It is a person's sex that defines whether they are male or female. Avoid gender in this context.

sexed up This phrase was overused in the first years of the century, and has burnt itself out. Avoid.

Shakespeare, William The greatest poet and dramatist in the English language, and a formidable neologist (borrower or creator of new words). He added extensively to English idiom, coining phrases that have endured intact into modern English nearly 400 years after his death in 1616. Consider these lines: 'I shall not look upon his like again,' 'more in sorrow than in anger,' 'Something is rotten in the state,' 'Murder most foul,' 'Brevity is the soul of wit,' 'The play's the thing.' These half-dozen immortal phrases are all from just one act of one play (Hamlet, II) – which helps gives some idea of the scale of Shakespeare's unique contribution to the English we speak now, and always will.

Shall and **will** In the 21st century, the auxiliary verb 'shall' will doubtless continue what has already been a long journey into oblivion. Somehow, the word has come to seem old-fashioned. There are really no longer any rules of grammar governing which to use, but there are still places in which shall really does a better job. An example is "I'll go to the pub, shall I?" This is quite a different question to "I'll go to the pub, will I?" because the first version implies a sense of choice, and the second makes it seem the speaker is destined to go the pub whatever happens. As always,

shear and sheer

when choosing the right word, be sure it makes real sense before committing yourself to it.

shear and **sheer** The verb to shear means to cut or trim. Sheer is an adjective meaning pure or absolute as in 'sheer luck' or very steep as in 'a sheer drop.'

shoo-in A recently revived American English term for a very easy task, as "the election was a shoo-in."

should and **would** In just the same way that 'shall' is diminishingly used, so is 'should' – with 'would' filling the void. It used to be the convention that 'should' was used in the first person, thus "I should" and "we should" and "would" for second or third persons, but this nicety is now fading. But in one sense, 'should' should be retained. It is in connection with duty or obligation, as in "Should I go and visit her today?" and "I should go at once." In this sort of context, 'would' would certainly not do.

show business Two words, but showbiz as one.

shriek Journalistic jargon for an exclamation mark (!).

sibilant In phonetics, the sound made by the pronunciation of the letter 's.'

sic It's Latin for 'true' and is placed in brackets after a word that has been deliberately misspelled or misused, usually because it is a quotation.

silent consonant A letter left unpronounced, as in dou<u>b</u>t, <u>p</u>salm and recei<u>p</u>t. Why have these curiosities survived into the 21st century? Blame the Renaissance. As the influence of the Classical world was revived in the 15th century, scholars of English desired to remind their readers that most of the words in the language originated in Latin and Greek. To show off their knowledge that doubt, then spelled 'dout' because it came into medieval English via French *doute*, derived originally from Latin *dubitare* they added the b – and it stuck. In its way, it was a nationalistic gesture, reasserting the Classical origins of English over the Dutch, French, German and Norse influences of the intervening millennium since Roman influence waned in Britain from the fifth century and Anglo-Saxon languages began to infiltrate.

simile Figure of speech in which one thing is described by comparing it with something quite different. The phrase usually incorporates 'as' or 'like' as in, "your eyes are like pools" or "cool as a mountain stream." Latin *similis* (like).

sincerely In signing off a formal letter, use 'yours sincerely' if you have addressed the recipient by name. See faithfully.

singe In the participle, use singeing, not singing.

singular In grammar, a word or word form denoting a single person. "I am" is the first person singular of the verb 'to be.'

skyglow One of the third millennium's most worrisome sources of environmental pollution, skyglow is the permanent light cast by streetlighting, depriving city dwellers of any opportunity to see the night sky and stars, and reportedly damaging the rhythms of many forms of plant and animal life.

SMS Short message service, the medium for messages sent between mobile phones.

snafu This bizarre acronym has unexpectedly survived into the 21st century. It means 'in total chaos' from the phrase 'situation normal: all fouled (or fucked) up.'

solecism A grammatical absurdity or a statement that makes no sense (see Bushisms). Not to be confused with solipsism, the theory that the existence of self is the only certainty. French, from Greek *soloikos* (speaking incorrectly).

soliloquy A speech made alone. Note spelling.

solipsism In philosophy, the theory that existence of self is the only certainty. From Latin *solus* (alone) and *ipse* (self). Beware confusion with solecism (*qv*).

soll- A useful spelling tip is that there is no common English word that starts 'soll-.' All words beginning with the phoneme (distinct word sound) 'sol' have a single 'l'.

sometime and **some time** The two are quite distinct. Sometime means former, as in "adventurer and sometime merchant banker Giles Hogg." Some time means at an indeterminate time, as in "we'll meet up again some time."

sonnet   A poem of 14 lines.

souped-up   Slang for enhanced or fortified, as in car with a souped-up engine. Origin of the phrase has not been established. It may be due to similarity with 'supercharged' or refer to the use of a particularly combustible – thus 'soupy' – fuel.

South East and **South West**   See compass points.

sow   To plant or scatter seed, as distinct from the verb to sew, to stitch with needle and thread.

spacers   Spacers are the sounds, words or phrases we all use in conversation, often subconsciously, to allow ourselves time to think of what to say next. They start with the likes of er, um and hmm, progress to actually, basically, innit, you know and well, then go all the way to at this moment in time, know what I mean and I said to him, I said. Except in reported speech, all these must be expressly avoided in written work.

speech marks   See quotation marks.

spelling   The choice and arrangement of the letters that form words is a function of written language that is as old as written language itself. Conventions in spelling have really only existed in the present sense in English since William Caxton produced the first printed book in the language in 1474. It was entitled the *Recuyell of the Historyes of Troye*. Ever since, the entire point of standardised spelling has been to make the written language comprehensible to the greatest number of people. For this reason, spelling evolves and, eventually, simplifies. But the convention remains. If you wish to be understood, spell words in the way the greatest number of people will recognise – and if that means looking up the words in the dictionary, so be it.

spiv   Mid-20th-century term of abuse for an uncouth male, usually flashily dressed. It has widened its scope to embrace all kinds of minor criminal and is used in upper-middle-class circles to deride highly paid members of disdained occupations including financial services and privatised utilities. Probably derives from American term spiff, meaning smartly turned out.

split infinitive Once a heresy, this is now common. The phrase "to boldly go," in the introductory voiceover to the eternal TV series *Startrek* is surely the most famous split infinitive in the world. There's no going back.

spondulicks Lately revived buzz word for money, now often abbreviated to 'spon.' Origin is an ancient Greek word for cowrie shells, a greatly valued treasure in the Classical era. Students at Oxford University first adopted the term as slang for money in the 18th century.

spoonerism The transposition of letters or words. The name comes from that of the Revd William Spooner (1844–1930) who had the habit, unintentionally, and is supposed to have uttered phrases such as "a half-warmed fish" when he meant "a half-formed wish." Spoonerism remains a much-used device in contemporary comedy-writing – with mixed success.

stadium As a Latin word (the Romans adapted it from Greek *stadion*) it can be correctly pluralized just as it was in Latin – as stadia. But this doesn't make it incorrect to use the plural stadiums, because stadium is now an English word, and this is the way we do our plurals.

stationary and **stationery** Stationary is an adjective meaning standing still, as in "the car was stationary when it was struck." Stationery is a noun for office papers and accessories, as in 'a stationery shop.'

stereotype Avoid stereotypes, especially when writing about real people. No sensible person really wants to be described as a "battling granny," a "fearless firefighter," or a "bored housewife." And not all Muslims are fundamentalist, nor are all Americans rich.

Stone Age You can use it loosely, as in 'Stone Age technology' for something outdated. But if referring to the period, note that it is the last of prehistory, when implements were still made entirely from stone. It immediately precedes the Bronze Age, when the first metal utensils and weapons came into use.

straight and strait Straight is an adjective meaning without a bend, literally or metaphorically. A strait is a narrow extent of water and in the plural, a state of affairs defined by a degree of trouble, as in 'dire straits.' Two words, straitjacket and strait-laced, originated from the narrow sense of the original strait, but some 21st-century dictionaries give straightjacket and straight-laced as alternatives. Stick to the original.

style   In newspaper and periodical publishing 'style' stands for consistency. Because there are different spellings for so many words, a 'style book' or sheet is issued to staff and contributors to clarify as many words or phrases as possible. Also laid down are rules for punctuation and use of italic type faces for foreign-language words, book, film or other titles – such as those of the newspaper when referring to itself.

sub-   The prefix indicates that the word probably refers to something below, either physically, or in degree of importance as in submarine or subordinate. Latin *sub* (under).

subject   In grammar, the noun or pronoun that predicates a sentence. In "I am here," 'I' is the subject of the sentence.

subjective   A subjective point of view is one held by a given person from their own standpoint, in other words a selfish point of view. An objective point of view is the opposite, and thus a disinterested one.

subjunctive   The mood of a verb used to denote something hoped for or wished, or merely something that might happen. In the phrase "if I were you," 'were' is in the subjunctive mood of the verb 'to be.' Professor Norman Stone, reviewing a book for *The Sunday Times* in 2001 on the alleged triumph of Western civilisation over Eastern, maintained that earlier books proposing this notion claimed that "the Indo-Europeans were distinguished from other races because they used the subjunctive and knew about agriculture." I hope this is of some help.

subordinate clause   In a sentence, an inserted additional phrase that introduces a complementary or supplementary theme. In "The bus came along, and he got on it." 'he got on it' is the subordinate clause, as introduced into the sentence by the conjunction 'and.'

super The prefix indicates that the word probably refers to something above, either physically, or in degree of importance, as in superstore or supervisor. Latin *super* (above).

supersede Note spelling is not 'supercede.'

swap or **swop** The form swap is closer to the word's origin, Middle English *swappen*, meaning to strike (as in slap) and later to strike a bargain, but dictionaries consistently give both spellings as acceptable.

suffix An add-on to a word, modifying it, as in the suffix '-able' added to 'love.'

surgeon A doctor who carries out manual operations on patients, but also the name given to a more-general physician in military service, as a navy surgeon. Practising surgeons are commonly known by the appropriate title Miss/Mr/Mrs/Ms rather than as Dr, but surgeons who have the highest university degree in their profession, a doctorate in surgery, may use the title Dr. Confusingly, the initials conferred by the doctorate are DCh, recalling the earlier form 'chirurgeon' from Greek *cheirourgos* (a manual worker).

surreal Used loosely to mean dream-like, as in "it was a surreal experience," it derives from the 20th-century surrealist school of art, which took as its theme the workings of the subconscious.

Sword of Damocles See Damocles.

syllable Word sound. Every word is composed of one or more syllables.

syllepsis Figure of speech in which one word introduces two separate ideas, as in "she gave him a cup of tea and a hostile look."

syllogism An invalid form of reason in which parallel ideas are falsely made to meet, as in "all cows are animals, therefore all animals are cows."

sympathy See empathy.

syn- Words beginning with this prefix commonly have meanings connected to likeness or togetherness. Greek *sun* (with).

synecdoche

synecdoche   Figure of speech in which the whole of an idea is taken for the part, or vice versa. An example is: "England defeats Australia" in, say, a cricket match. Apart from the absurdity of the premise, the statement is a synecdoche because it contracts the description of English and Australian cricket teams to the point of asserting the entirety of each nation was pitched one against the other on this sporting occasion. Greek *sun* (together) and *ekdechestai* (to receive).

synonym   A word with the same meaning as another. 'Big' and 'large' are synonyms.

synopsis   An outline or summary of a longer work.

syntax   Dread word for students of English. It is the set of criteria by which use of the language can be judged correct, or otherwise. The sentence, 'The cat sat on the mat' is correct syntax, being a conventional arrangement of subject, verb and object, clearly setting out the relationships between all the words and thus conveying sense. Greek *sun* (together) and *tassein* (to arrange).

syringe   In the participle, use syringeing, not syringing.

T

tautology The repetition of the same idea or item of information within one phrase. An example is "visitors are restricted only to the public areas," as the 'only' is redundant. Greek *to auto* (the same).

team and **teem** The noun team means a group that work or play together. The verb teem means to be numerous, as "the river teems with fish."

tec and **tech** Both are short for technical, technology etc, but in phrases such as hi-tech, the spelling with the 'h' is still dominant. Long ago, in the 20th century, 'tec' was a common abbreviation of detective.

Technicolor A common word, but a trade name. Use the initial capital and American spelling.

tectonic Buzz word used to suggest any newsworthy event, either as a noun ("summer is not the season for tectonics") or adjectivally ("a tectonic performance"). From continental and oceanic tectonic plates forming the Earth's crust, whose movements can cause earthquakes.

ten Write as ten, not 10, in keeping with the style guide to spell out all figures nought/zero to ten.

Teutonic The vaguely derogatory term Teutonic for a German makes no sense. History identifies the Teutons as populating Jutland, now in Scandinavia, in the 4th century BC. The Latin word *Teutoni* is of Indo-European origin and merely means 'people.'

text message A new, although largely derivative, vocabulary is building up from the abbreviations, contractions and acronyms used in the short messages sent to mobile phones. Below are a few of the more familiar examples.

text message

AAMOF – As a matter of fact

AFAIC – As far as I'm concerned

AFAICT – As far as I can tell

AFAIK – As far as I know

AFK – Away from keyboard

ASAP – As soon as possible

ATK – At the keyboard

BAK – Back at keyboard

BBL – Be back later

BCOS – Because

BFN or B4N – Bye for now

BITMT – But in the meantime

BOT – Back on topic

BRB – Be right back

BRT – Be right there

BTW – By the way

C4N – Ciao for now

CON – Call of nature

COS – Because

CRS – Can't remember 'stuff'

CU – See you

CWOT – Complete waste of time

CYA – See you

DITYID – Did I tell you I'm distressed?

DIY – Do it yourself

DNT – Don't

DYNO – Do you know?

EOD – End of discussion

EZ – Easy

F – Female

F2F – Face to face

FAQ – Frequently asked questions

FBOW – For better or worse

FOAF – Friend of a friend

FOCL – Falling off chair laughing

FWIW – For what it's worth

FYA – For your amusement

FYI – For your information

GA – Go ahead

GAL – Get a life

GBTW – Get back to work

GFC – Going for coffee

GFETE – Grinning from ear to ear

GLB4UGH – Get lost before you get hurt

GMTA – Great minds think alike

GR&D – Grinning, running & ducking

GR8 – Great

GTG – Got to go

GTGN – Got to go now

GTGTTBR – Got to go to the bathroom

GTRM – Going to read mail

GTTL – Gone to the loo

HAND – Have a nice day

HHOK – Ha ha only kidding

HTH – Hope this helps

IAC – In any case

IAE – In any event

IASA – I am so annoyed

IC – I see

IDGI – I don't get it

IMCO – In my considered opinion

IMHO – In my humble opinion

IMNSHO – In my not so humble opinion

IMO – In my opinion

IMPE – In my previous / personal experience

IMVHO – In my very humble opinion

IOTTMCO – Intuitively obvious to the most casual observer

IOW – In other words

IRL – In real life

ISP – Internet service provider

IYKWIM – If you know what I mean

J/K – Just kidding

JIC – Just in case

KISS – Keep it simple stupid

L8R – Later

LD – Later dude

LOL – Laughing out loud or Lots of love

LTNS – Long time no see

M – Male

MTPW – My two pennyworth

NE – Any

No1 – No one

NRN – No reply necessary

OIC – Oh I see

OLL – Online love

OMDB – Over my dead body

ONNA – Oh no, not again!

OOO – Out of order

OTF – On the floor

OTOH – On the other hand

OTTOMH – Off the top of my head

PCMCIA – People can't memorize computer industry acronyms

PLS – Please

POS – Parents over shoulder

PU – That stinks!

REHI – Hello again

ROE – Raising one eyebrow

ROTF – Rolling on the floor

ROFL – Rolling on the floor laughing

RSN – Real soon now

RTDOX – Read the documentation / directions

RTFM – Read the fucking manual

RUOK – Are you OK?

SI – Sarcasm intended

SNAFU – Situation normal; all fouled up

SO – Significant other

SOL – Smiling out loud (or You're out of luck)

SOMY? – Sick of me yet?

SS ><)))"> – Something smells fishy

SSTM – Smiling smugly to myself

SUM1 – someone

SWL – Squeals with laughter

TAFN – That's all for now

TANSTAAFL – There ain't no such thing as a free lunch

TEOTWAWKI – The end of the world as we know it

THX – Thanks

TIA – Thanks In advance

TLK2UL8R – Talk to you later

TMK – To my knowledge

2U2 – To you too

text message

TPTB – The powers that be

TRDF – Tears rolling down my face

TSWC – Tell someone who cares

TTBOMK – To the best of my knowledge

TTFN – Ta-ta for now!

TTYL – Talk to you later

TWIMC – To whom it may concern

TXL – Thanks loads

Txs – Thanks

URJ – You are joking

URL – Web page address

w/o – Without

WB – Welcome Back

Wens – When is

WI – With irony

WOMBAT – Waste of money, brain and time

WRT – With regard to

WTG – Way to go!

WU? – What's up?

WWW – World wide web

WYBMADIITY – Will you buy me a drink if I tell you?

WYSIWYG – What you see is what you get

YGIAGAM – Your guess is as good as mine

YGWYPF – You get what you pay for

YMMV – Your mileage may vary

YR – Yeah

thank you   Two words.

that   Is the phrase 'I think you are beautiful' somehow enhanced by extension to 'I think that you are beautiful'? Surely not. Dispense with 'that' in this context. It is less easy to be firm about the use in the function of a relative pronoun of 'that' as opposed to 'which.' In the sentence "the car that he most wanted was a Ferrari" would the sense be improved by substituting the word 'which'? In terms of the conventions of grammar, you can have it either way. But when the pronoun is personal, it's different. "The man that's coming to mend the washing machine" is too impersonal. "The man who's coming … " is more friendly.

the   Definite article and the most-used word in written English.

themselves   The plural personal pronoun has now come into universal use to obviate gender specificity (*qv*), even in the singular. This is the British *Reader's Digest* offering ironic advice on how to "get rid of bad dinner date" in 2001: "Pull out a harmonica and play the blues while your date talks about themselves." There must be a better way.

then Don't use this word as a conjunction to denote consequentiality. When one part of a sentence relates the effect of what is described in the other part, the whole should be written in a way that makes a connecting 'then' redundant. For example this phrase from an erratum added to a 2000 A level English paper (OCR) ran: "If this is the case then you can ignore the rest of this notice." The word 'then' is superfluous, and bad English.

third person The third person singular is 'he' or 'she' and the third person plural is 'they.'

titles In print the names of publications, plays, films and so on are commonly set in italics – as "according to an article in *The Sun* yesterday" or "Julie Walters starred in *Harry Potter*."

tmesis A fun grammatical device in which a word is split and another word or phrase inserted to create a more emphatic version of the original. Usually jocular, as in 'abso-bloody-lutely.' Greek *temno* (to cut).

toponym A place name – the Arctic Circle, New York, France – or a word coined in association with the name of a place, real or imaginary. Examples are arcadian, bohemian, calico, cashmere, caucasian, champagne, china, chivvy, elysian, laconic, madeira, millinery, port, spartan, utopian. Greek *topos* (place) and *onoma* (name).

touchy-feely A recent term of contempt for any sentimental behaviour or pronouncement.

trademark If a word is a trademark, such as Coca-Cola, Jaguar or Zanussi, it must be written with an initial capital letter, and may not be used in a generic sense. Some trademark owners are notoriously litigious and may seek redress if their name is taken in vain.

transitive See intransitive

travesty Popular word with trades unionists, who like to describe pay offers from employers as "an absolute travesty." The word means an absurd or monstrous representation, as "the witness's statement was a travesty of the truth." Its original 17th-century function was to describe someone dressed in a grotesque costume such as a clown's outfit. From French *travestir* (to disguise).

trek Oft-misspelled. It's a South African word, meaning to pull a wagon (with an ox) and now in a wider context to go on an arduous journey – or the arduous journey itself. Note spellings trekker, trekking etc.

trilogy A work in three parts, usually literary, but occasionally dramatic or cinematic.

trooper and **trouper** A trooper is an enlisted man in a cavalry regiment. A trouper is a member of troupe, a team of dancers or other performers. It is the latter who figures in the phrase "she's a real trouper," for someone with notable appetite, fortitude or *esprit de corps*.

trustafarian Recent blended word for a wealthy young person about town, able to afford an extravagant and unproductive lifestyle thanks to the income from a trust fund.

tsar See czar.

tsunami This marine phenomenon, in which convulsive movements of the seabed cause huge and destructive waves, has lately been adopted as a metaphor for any overwhelming action, as in 'a tsunami of unwelcome publicity.' Japanese for 'harbour wave.'

Tudor It describes the period in English history defined by the reigns of the Tudor monarchs, starting in 1485 with Henry VII's accession and ending in 1603 with the death of Elizabeth I. It also refers to a style of architecture of the day that featured gables and exposed timberwork – thus the 'mock-Tudor' style of some subsequent architecture.

tweeny Formerly a housemaid – from 'between the stairs' signifying a servant seen in the formal part of the house as well as downstairs in the kitchen – this term (also spelled tweenie) now denotes children aged between 8 and 12.

24/7 Current contraction blending '24 hours a day' with 'seven days a week.' As, "he worked 24/7 to prepare for his exams."

txtmsg This 'e-bbreviation' of 'text message' – a keyed message sent between computers and/or mobile phones – stands for a recent vocabulary of abbreviations and contractions devised for simplified communication in electronic media. One guide to this new e-language, *The Total Txtmsg Dictionary* (Michael O'Mara Books, 2001) has more than 10,000 entries.

U

-um Many words with this suffix are descended from Latin. For words directly derived, there has long been a case for using the Latin plural form, as referendum/referenda, stadium/stadia. But in the 21st century this practice is beginning to look old-fashioned. If you feel self-conscious about the Latin plural, don't use it.

umbrage Note the spelling. The word means a sense of injury or offence as in, "she took umbrage at his words" and originates from Latin *umbra* (shade).

under way The phrase, as in 'the project is under way,' is written as two words. Avoid the invented word 'underway', which is municipal-authority slang for an urban passageway beneath a road.

uninterested Beware confusion with disinterested. Uninterested means not interested, as in "he was uninterested in the subject." Disinterested means having no material connection, as in "he was a disinterested party to the affair."

unparliamentary The British Parliament's conventions forbid members from using abusive words in the debating chambers. MPs may not directly accuse each other of lying, of criminality, even of hypocrisy – at least not in so many words. Consequently, members have evolved artful phrases which, while not 'unparliamentary' in the strict sense are nevertheless calculated to give grave offence to opponents.

Contrary to the impression sometimes given in broadcasts of the proceedings of Parliament, MPs do not address each other across the floor of the House of Commons. All speeches, questions and responses are addressed to the Speaker, and members may only refer to their colleagues by their ministerial titles or via the names of their constituencies. It is unparliamentary for any member, other than the Speaker, to call an MP by his or her name. Members of the Privy Council (the

Cabinet and the Leader of the Opposition) are addressed as Right Honourable Members and all others as Honourable Members. Thus, 'My Right Honourable friend the Chancellor of the Exchequer' and 'the Honourable Member for Ipswich South.'

Unwinese　The nonsense language of British comedian Stanley Unwin (1911–2002) may not have made its way into the dictionaries, but deserves a place in linguistic history. Unwin attributed his habit of suddenly breaking into an incomprehensible babble to a remark made to him by his mother. Mrs Unwin had returned home from shopping one day with the news she had fallen off the bus and hurt her knee, and told it in these words: "I fallolopped and grazed my kneeclapper." Stanley protested that there were no such words, but his mother insisted they served her purpose. Stanley, who worked as a BBC radio reporter in the 1940s and 50s, took up the cause and made a good living from his recitations in films, on television and in countless stage performances. In his story-telling mode, he was wont to begin something like this: "Once a polly tie lode, when our young worle was fresh in univerbs and England its beauty garden, a young man set out in the early mordee ... " Unwin's familiar words of farewell were "Good lee bye-lode."

upon　Rarely can the word 'upon' now be used when 'on' will do. "Upon my word" would be an exception, but for the fact that no one uses the expression any more.

upper case　Another way of saying capital, as in letter.

US　Some newspapers prefer to print the initials for the United States with full points – U.S. – for fear of causing confusion with 'us' in headlines such as POPE FLIES INTO US. But this problem hardly arises in any other circumstances, and it makes sense to be consistent with other initial uses – UK, UN etc. Avoid full points in abbreviations whenever possible.

USA　As an initial representation for the United States of America, USA is waning. US is now very much more common in the English-speaking world.

USSR

USSR Union of Soviet Socialist Republics. It ceased to exist in 1991 after the resignation of the last Soviet president, Mikhail Gorbachev, and the abolition of the Communist Party, in favour of the nation's first democratically elected Head of State, Boris Yeltsin. The former union of 15 republics – of which Russia comprised three-quarters of the land area and half the total population – has now entirely disintegrated into sovereign democracies including Armenia, Georgia, Kazakhstan, Moldavia, Ukraine and Baltic states Estonia, Latvia and Lithuania. 'Russia' – a former misnomer for the Soviet Union as a whole – is now a separate democratic republic, still incorporating numerous distinct regions formerly known as autonomous Soviet republics, autonomous regions and national districts.

V

valediction   Farewell. An old-fashioned but picturesque word for goodbye. Latin *vale* (farewell) and *dicere* (to say).

venal and **venial**   Beware confusion between these two words. Venal describes behaviour conditioned by susceptibility to bribery, from Latin *venum* (item for sale).

Venial is a word from Christian theology (*qv*), denoting an act that is sinful, but not so sinful it will deprive the perpetrator of a place in Heaven. Venal sins are contrasted with mortal sins. Latin *venia* (forgiveness).

venereal   Relating to sexual desire or sexual intercourse. Thus, diseases such as gonorrhoea are known as venereal because they are sexually transmitted. Latin *venus* (sexual love).

vernacular   The language of a particular group, region or nation, particularly as spoken rather than formally written. Latin *vernaculus* (native).

Victorian   Strictly speaking, a period of British history defined by the reign of the last Hanoverian monarch, Queen Victoria, from 1837 to 1901. Expansion of industry and empire accompanied by the emergence of a prosperous middle class during the period have given the term Victorian some confusing meanings. 'Victorian values' can refer to the hard-work ethic of the time, but might also describe either a kind of hypocritical primness or the heartlessness with which some prosperous Victorians are believed to have treated their less-fortunate contemporaries. Conditions in hospitals, schools and prisons are frequently damned as 'Victorian' in the media – and yet the countless reforms of the period did improve social conditions (in a time of unprecedented population growth) to an extent never previously attempted. It is worth remembering that the reign saw the abolition of slavery, the extension of voting rights (though not to women) and the

Victorian

rapid expansion of public health care and education as well as mass transport (railways). Most of today's public institutions devoted to national culture – museums, galleries and theatres – date from the period. Beware confusing 'Victorian' with the bleak 'Dickensian' memory we retain of urban poverty and moral degeneracy supplied by the period's leading novelist.

weasel word   A word that is misapplied or ambiguous. Many buzz words, such as 'parameter' and 'quantum leap' are weasel words, so distanced by popular misuse that they are entirely divorced from their true meanings. Avoid all weasel words.

weblish   Recent term for the shorthand English, largely without capital letters and punctuation, used on the Internet and in e-communications.

welch and **welsh**   These two verbs both mean to break a promise or rat on a deal, as in "he welched on the bet." The variant 'welch' is the more recent spelling, but seems likely to be the front runner, as it avoids giving offence to that fine and upstanding race, the Welsh.

whassup   Recent contraction of 'what's up' adapted as an advertising catchword by the producers of American Budweiser beer for a UK television campaign launched in 2000. Within days of the first broadcasts of the commercials, the word was in widespread use.

which   See that.

whinge   Note spelling, with the 'h.' In participle, use whingeing, not whinging.

Whodunit   A detective mystery. Note spelling.

whom   The objective case of 'who.' Don't be afraid to use 'whom' as it can be important in keeping the sense of a sentence. In familiar phrases such as "To whom it may concern," substituting an incorrect 'who' could diminish employment prospects.

whose   Possessive pronoun; as in, 'whose car is this?' Beware confusion of the kind illustrated in a broadsheet newspaper report about Prince William: 'A boy who moves like someone whose been cuddled a lot.' The writer meant to say 'who's' – as a contraction of 'who has.'

wile   As a noun, usually in the plural, it means a cunning lure or stratagem, as in "he was trapped by her wiles." But it can also be used as a verb meaning to lure or entice, as in "she wiled him away from his wife." Beware confusion with the verb to 'while,' which means to pass time, as "she whiled away the hours wondering how she might wile her lover away from his wife."

will   See shall.

won't   Abbreviation of 'will not' must be written with apostrophe.

wont   Habit or custom; as "it was his wont to eat a kipper for breakfast." An old-fashioned word usually used in a jocular mood. Do not confuse with 'won't.'

words   Don't use too many. A *Guardian* newspaper report about a 2001 survey on regional differences in income around Britain said: "The survey does not detail the causes behind why those areas that have the most wealth are doing best."

World Trade Center   The twin-towered office complex in Manhattan, New York, destroyed in a terrorist attack on 11 September 2001. UK publishers mostly use the English spelling Centre.

world war   The Great War in Europe of 1914–18 has been known as the First World War since its horrors were eclipsed by those of the next war in Europe from 1939–45, and called the Second World War. The terms World War One (or I) and World War Two or (II) are American, but now widely used on both sides of the Atlantic.

would   See should.

wrack   There is no need to use this word in everyday writing. See rack.

wreak   Meaning to cause, as in "storms wreak havoc," this verb is written as 'wreaked' in the past tense. The word 'wrought' – an old past participle of the verb 'to work' – is unconnected, and the word 'wraught,' which has been known to appear in print, simply does not exist.

WWF   The former World Wildlife Fund is now the Worldwide Fund for Nature, but continues to be known as the WWF.

X

-x Some French words commonly used in English have the plural ending -x. Should this form be used when using these words in an English context? Examples are bureau, château and purlieu. The rule to follow is based on pronunciation. If the word is commonly pronounced in English just as it is in French – as in bureau and château – write the plural form with the French ending: bureaux, châteaux. Where the pronunciation is English – purlieu as 'perleeoo' rather than French 'poorleeyuh' – write the English plural form, purlieus.

-x- *versus* **-ct-** Which is correct, connection or connexion, inflection or inflexion? Dictionaries give both spellings of these and a handful of other nouns ending -ion and adjectives ending -ive. Best advice is to play safe and stick to the -ct- version, because the great majority of relevant words follow this form, taking it from their verb root – correction, direction etc – and the form is acceptable for all nouns derived from verbs in the same way. The few words that take only the -x- form, such as crucifixion (from crucify), have different verb roots.

xenophobia Fear or hatred of foreigners. Now becoming a politically correct way of saying 'racism.'

Xmas Traditionalists express indignation at the shortening of the word Christmas, denouncing it as a modern heresy. But it is not so modern as all that. This is from celebrated Somerset diarist Rev James Woodforde's entry for 25 December 1764: "Fifteen poor old people dined here as usual being Xmas Day." The Oxford dictionaries state that the first written evidence of this "common abbreviation" dates from 1551.

Y

YBA Young British Artists. Members include Tracy Emin, Damien Hirst, Rachel Whiteread and others who have come to prominence in conceptual and associated art forms since the 1980s.

yob Backslang for a young lout. Use of the term is now largely confined to educated middle-class speakers, so must be avoided by those seeking to establish working-class credentials through their choice of vocabulary.

-yse Use only this verb ending for analyse, paralyse etc. Analyze, paralyze etc are American spellings.

Z

Zeitgeist This trendy word, meaning the 'spirit of the time' – from *Zeit* (time) and *Geist* (spirit) – is German. As with all German nouns, it should correctly be written with an initial capital letter.

zeugma A fun figure of speech in which one word refers to two or more others in different senses, as in 'ladies in tight frocks and evident discomfort.' Greek *zeugnunai* (to yoke together).

zigzag One word.

Zimmer Use the initial capital. The Zimmer walking frame is trademarked.

zoology It is correctly pronounced 'zoh ology.' 'Zoo ology' would be right only if the word were spelt zooology. Greek *zoion* (animal) and *logos* (word).

Acknowledgements

The author gives thanks to the following for suggestions and observations made to me in the course of compiling this book:

Steve Barnes, Peter Booth, Andrew Campbell, Adam Constantine, Eric Crees, Pepsy Denning, Marcus FitzGibbon, Caromay Gifford, Sheila Halley, Max Halley, Laelia Hartnoll, Mario Reading, Leopold von Bülow Quirk, Michael Randolph, Vaughan Williams, Mike Wren.